LIFE WITHOUT PAROLE

Living in Prison Today

Victor Hassine
Inmate AM4737
Pennsylvania Department of Corrections

Edited by
Thomas J. Bernard
Pennsylvania State University

and

Richard McCleary
University of California, Irvine

Foreword by
John Irwin
San Francisco State University

Afterword by
Richard A. Wright
University of Scranton

Roxbury Publishing Company
Los Angeles, California

Library of Congress Cataloging-in-Publication Data:

Hassine, Victor, 1955-
Life without parole: living in prison today / Victor Hassine; edited by
    Thomas J. Bernard, Richard McCleary; foreword by John Irwin;
    afterword by Richard A. Wright.
    p. cm.
    ISBN 0-935732-76-4 (alk. paper)
    1. Prisoners—Pennsylvania—Case studies. 2. Hassine, Victor,1955- . 3.
    Life imprisonment—Pennsylvania—Case studies.
    4. Prisons—Pennsylvania—Case studies. 5. Graterford State Correctional
    Institution. I. Bernard, Thomas J. II. McCleary, Richard. III. Title.
    HV9475.P2H37 1996   95-48102
    365'.6'0922748—dc20   CIP

LIFE WITHOUT PAROLE: LIVING IN PRISON TODAY

Publisher and Editor: Claude Teweles
Developmental Editor: Anton Diether
Assistant Editors: Dawn VanDercreek and Joyce Rappaport
Production: James Ballinger
Cover Design: Marnie Deacon
Cover Photograph: Byron Wright*
Typography: Synergistic Data Systems

*The cover photograph of the State Correctional Institution at Graterford was
taken with the permission of that institution.

> Note: All author royalties for this book are being donated directly to The
> Families of Murder Victims Program, a nonprofit organization affiliated with
> the Antiviolence Partnership of Philadelphia, Pennsylvania.

Printed on acid-free paper in the United States of America. This paper meets the
standards for recycling of the Environmental Protection Agency.

ISBN: 0-935732-76-4

ROXBURY PUBLISHING COMPANY
P.O. Box 491044
Los Angeles, California 90049-9044
(213) 653-1068 Fax: (213) 653-4140
Email: roxbury@crl.com

This book is dedicated to the fond memory of Lenny and Ester Silverman and Sandra Wolfe Karlin, three people whose selfless acts of loving kindness have shown me the way.

Table of Contents

Acknowledgements vii

Preface: *The Story Behind This Book* x
    by *Thomas J. Bernard*

Foreword xiv
    by *John Irwin*

About the Author xv

PART I: PRISON LIFE

Introduction 3

Chapter 1: How I Became a Convict 5

Chapter 2: Things Missed 17

Chapter 3: Prison Violence 27

Chapter 4: The Underground Economy 35

Chapter 5: Prison Politics 47

Chapter 6: Race Relations in Prison 59

Chapter 7: Saying Goodbye 67

PART II: INTERVIEWS

Chapter 8: David: A Sexual Victim 71

Chapter 9: Chaser: A Medication Addict 77

Chapter 10: Toney: An AIDS Tragedy 85

Chapter 11: Albert Brown: A Permanent Resident 91

Chapter 12: Jacko: Surviving the Hole 99

PART III: OP ED

Chapter 13: Prison Overcrowding 107

Chapter 14: Homosexuality: The Pink Cells 111

Chapter 15: Relationships Between Inmates
   and Guards 117

Chapter 16: A Theory of Prison Evolution 121

Chapter 17: Conclusion: The Runaway Train 125

Afterword 129
   by *Richard A. Wright*

APPENDICES

Appendix A: Mr. Smith Goes to Harrisburg 143

Appendix B: 'A State Tries to Rein in a Prison
   Awash in Drugs' 155
   Reprinted from *The New York Times*

Acknowledgements

I owe a lifetime of gratitude to a great many people who supported me, cared about me, believed in me, and encouraged me during these difficult prison years. You can't do time in prison alone and still expect to come out of it sane. I needed a lot of help from people on the outside to constantly remind me that I was still a worthwhile part of the American quilt.

I would like to start by thanking my father, mother, and brother who in many ways did this time with me so I would never have to feel completely alone. I hope the publication of this book will give them that sense of pride which I have not been able to offer since my incarceration. But for them I would have long ago lost this struggle to retain my dignity.

I would like to personally thank Deborah Anthony who not only saved my life but also rescued my heart and my love.

From Graterford Penitentiary I would like to thank Larry Karlin for being the devoted friend I could always count on to be in my corner; Ted Klugman (Tefka), who was the first one to encourage me to write about my prison experiences and who introduced me to the Fortune Society and the Pen Prison Writing Contest; Phil and Frida Zelt, Catherine Sion, Itka Zigmantovitch, and many other prison volunteers who showed me friendship, kindness, and concern, which in turn gave me the strength and inspiration to write this book; Angus Love, the best, most honest, and committed lawyer I know, without whose dedication Pennsylvania prisons would be much worse places to be; and Irv Hommer, the radio talk-show host who showed me in no uncertain terms that many people out there really do care.

From Western Penitentiary I would like to thank Meyer and Sandra Tattelman, Sam Steinberg, and Rabbi Epstein—Jewish volunteers who managed to inspire hope in the most hopeless prison imaginable; Ken Davenport who, with the assistance of Nelson

"Peepers" Mikesel, helped me to file and successfully litigate my conditions of confinement lawsuit against Western Penitentiary; Ed Feinstein, the lawyer whose skill and talent kept me many times from harm's way; and Bob Koehler, my college fraternity brother (Phi Alpha), who has stayed with me all these years.

From Rockview Penitentiary I would like to thank Rita Foderaro, a dear friend who believed in my talent and encouraged people to read my work; and two anonymous staff members who provided me with the encouragement and support to write this book. They both know who they are.

Many thanks to former Pennsylvania Commissioner of Corrections David Owens who tried diligently to change the Pennsylvania prison system for the better; former Commissioner of Corrections Joseph D. Lehman who gave not only his permission but his support for the writing of this book; the Pennsylvania Prison Society for having the courage and perseverance to demand a human face on the Pennsylvania Department of Corrections; the Fortune Society of New York for promoting the annual PEN American Prison Writing Competition, which was directly responsible for my decision to express myself through the written word.

Finally, a special thanks to the Superintendent of the State Correctional Institution at Rockview, Dr. Joseph F. Mazurkiewicz, for working so hard and unyieldingly to keep his prison safe and clean for its inmates. If I had been sent to Dr. Mazurkiewicz' prison fifteen years ago to serve my time, I probably would not have had very much to write about. And a very special thanks to Dr. Thomas J. Bernard and Dr. Richard McCleary for their patience and dedication to making all this possible and recognizing the need for this candid look into the heart of the criminal justice system. Lastly, my deepest gratitude to Sherry Truesdell of Truesdell Word Processing Services for her professionalism, honesty, and dependability; and to Roxbury publisher Claude Teweles and editor Anton Diether for their invaluable efforts in making this book a reality.

In addition, my publisher and I would like to offer thanks to the following individuals who read the first-draft manuscript of this book and provided so many useful suggestions: Leo Carroll (*University of Rhode Island*), Dean J. Champion (*Minot State Univer-*

sity), Paul Cromwell (*University of Miami*), John Irwin (*San Francisco State University*), Lucien X. Lombardo (*Old Dominion University*), Linda G. Smith (*Georgia State University*), Jon Sorenson (*University of Texas, Pan American*), and Richard A. Wright (*University of Scranton*).

Preface

The Story Behind This Book

Thomas J. Bernard
Pennsylvania State University

In December 1992, I received a call from the local representative of the Pennsylvania Prison Society, a private, voluntary agency that works with prisoners. She wanted to know if I would address the Lifers Group at the State Correctional Institution at Rockview about future possibilities for the release of life-sentenced inmates. Rockview is located near Pennsylvania State University, where I teach criminal justice courses.

"Lifers" are inmates who have been sentenced to life without parole. What these lifers wanted to know was whether there was any hope that they might eventually get out of prison. For them, the only way out (other than death or escape) is to receive a commutation from the governor. Up until about 1980, commutations in Pennsylvania were treated somewhat like parole. There were hearings on the issue, so that those who applied for commutation had at least some but not very much hope that it might be granted.

Since the recent shift to a "get-tough" approach to crime, however, this is no longer the case. In the first half of the 1970s, Pennsylvania averaged over 30 commutations per year. By the second half of the 1980s, that figure had dropped to just over one per year. At the same time, about 100 life-sentenced inmates were coming into Pennsylvania's system every year. So as a practical matter, life-sentenced inmates today can expect their requests for commutation to be denied, regardless of the circumstances of their crime, the length of time they have served, or their record and accomplishments since they have been in prison. This is not likely to change any time soon.

So my answer to the lifers' question was no. But I tried to couple that bleak message with a tiny glimmer of hope. Inmate population pressures in the Pennsylvania system, in my view, made it inevitable that a genuine consideration of commutation applications would eventually have to be resumed. There were simply too many life-sentenced inmates coming into the system, and the present commutation policy was too impractical to last forever.

If these inmates have nothing else in their lives, they have time. If they can do nothing else with their time, they can wait. The small shred of hope that I could give them was gratefully received. I was enthusiastically thanked for my presentation. Many smiling, desperately friendly faces were thrust into mine to tell me how much my talk meant to them.

One of those friendly faces belonged to Victor Hassine, although I did not remember meeting him at the time. Then in August 1993, an envelope arrived in the mail containing three of the interviews that are included in this book. A letter from Victor proposed that I share this material with my students since, "if they are to make a meaningful contribution to the administration of justice in Pennsylvania, they need to know the truth about its operation." I wrote him a brief note of thanks and then set the envelope aside.

Eventually, I got around to reading the material carefully. To my surprise, the interviews provided strikingly vivid descriptions of inmates and life in prison that were remarkably well-written and deeply insightful. I was intrigued. After considerable thought, I came to the conclusion that this material might form the basis for a book about prison life. I decided to look into it further.

First, I had to find out if the Department of Corrections would allow a book to be written by an inmate. It was a very long time before I received an answer: inmates could indeed write books as part of their freedom of speech. By the time I received their reply, Roxbury Publishing Company had agreed to publish the book.

On February 28, 1994, I wrote Victor a letter to inform him that I had been working on a proposal for him, that the Department of Corrections had agreed to the book, and that a publisher was ready to offer him a contract if he still wanted to do it. It was the first time I had communicated with him since my note of thanks, because I did not want to offer any good news until all the pieces were in place, for fear of raising his hopes prematurely.

Victor's response was ecstatic. He readily agreed to all the arrangements, suggesting that his royalties go to a Philadelphia group called "Families of Murder Victims." This seemed to be a very appropriate group to receive the author's profits, particularly from a book by a man sentenced to life imprisonment for first-degree murder.

"Families of Murder Victims" is a private, nonprofit agency housed in, but not affiliated with, the Philadelphia District Attorney's office. Its purpose is to help families of homicide victims cope with their grief and to assist them as their cases work their way through the legal system. Funding for the agency comes from the Victims of Crime Act, the Philadelphia District Attorney's office, and the United Way, as well as from private donations. The contract with Roxbury Publishing specified that all of Victor's royalties would go directly to this group.

In my view, the result of this process is a book that provides a penetrating and insightful look at prison life in America today. Whether you are for or against prison reform, whether you support or oppose the get-tough policy on criminals, this book will give you a first-hand experience of what prisons are really like—a revealing look at prison life from the *inside*.

We, as citizens of a democratic society, should know what prisons are all about. Our society makes an enormous investment in prisons as part of social policy. As of this writing, the United States has about 1,100,000 people incarcerated in adult federal and state correctional institutions. Another half million people are in local jails, with an additional 100,000 in secure juvenile institutions. This totals over 1,700,000 individuals behind bars in this country.

This number is unmatched anywhere else in the modern industrialized world and shows an astonishing increase over this country's imprisonment rates in the past. Before 1970, our imprisonment rate was relatively stable at around 100 sentenced inmates for every 100,000 Americans. In that year, we had about 200,000 inmates in federal and state adult prisons. But around 1970, the numbers began taking off. By the end of 1994, the total number of people in those prisons was just over 1,000,000 and the rate was about 400 sentenced inmates for every 100,000 Americans.[1]

At the present time, the total number of inmates in the country is growing at a rate of about 90,000 per year. That means that by the end of every week, correctional administrators in this country have to find rooms and beds for 1,700 more inmates in their prisons than they had at the beginning of the same week. This task is almost impossible, and it has led to many of the problems described in this book.

As responsible citizens, we need to ask ourselves whether this enormous investment in prisons is a worthy social policy. I hope that Victor Hassine's book will help to stimulate debate over this very serious question.

---

1. Bureau of Justice Statistics, "Prisoners in 1994." U.S. Government Printing Office, Washington DC, 1995.

Foreword

John Irwin
San Francisco State University

Victor Hassine's *Life Without Parole* takes its place among a rather large array of descriptions of prison life written by prisoners. Some of these were written in the last century, but the majority of them came about in the last three decades, for the obvious reason that prisoners are becoming more and more literate. Some of the best of these are: *In the Belly of the Beast* by Jack Abbott; *A Sense of Freedom* by Jimmy Boyle (a British prisoner); *Tales from the Joint* by K. Hawkeye Gross; and *The Big Huey* by Greg Newbold (a New Zealand prisoner).

I think Hassine's book is most like Gross' *Tales from the Joint,* because both books were written by people who had little experience with the social worlds, mostly lower class, that supply prisons their inmates. *Life Without Parole*'s particular strength is that it is about large, contemporary prisons. Until reading this book, I hadn't seen any good prisoner descriptions about prisons today, after the extreme overcrowding and the violence between prisoners that have changed conditions so significantly. Hassine has a sharp eye for contemporary prison violence because he came to prison as an outsider, unfamiliar with the patterns and values of the thieves, hustlers, drug addicts, state-raised convicts, and gang bangers who populate the prison. At times, perhaps, Hassine accepts too readily other prisoners' fairly standard explanations for the way things are, but he is intelligent and frequently sees things clearly from his very different perspective (he is a law-school graduate).

All in all, *Life Without Parole* is a very valuable work on the contemporary prison, produced by an intelligent individual who has experienced prison first-hand for an extended period.

About the Author

Born: June 20, 1955.

1956: Family exiled from Egypt for religious reasons.

1961: Family immigrated to Trenton, New Jersey.

1966: Became an American citizen.

1977: Graduated from Dickenson College, majoring in Political Science and History.

1980: June, graduated from New York Law School. November, arrested on an open charge of homicide.

1981: Convicted of first-degree murder and sent to SCI-Graterford.

1985: Helped to found the first prison synagogue.

1986: Helped to found the first Jewish Post-Release House. Filed conditions of confinement suit in Federal Court against SCI-Graterford to abolish double-celling. September, assaulted by an inmate and transferred to SCI-Pittsburgh.

1987: Filed conditions of confinement suit in Federal Court against SCI-Pittsburgh and Department of Corrections.

1989: January, assaulted by an inmate and recovered in outside hospital. April, transferred from Pittsburgh hospital to SCI-Camp Hill. August, transferred to SCI-Rockview.

1990: Received Pennsylvania Prison Society's Inmate of the Year Award.

Editor's Note

The names of many of the inmates and prison employees described in this book have been changed to protect their identity.

PART I

Prison Life

Editor's Note

In this first section, the author introduces himself and describes the beginning of his life as a convict in prison. His first life, which is briefly summarized above in "About the Author," ended in 1981 at the gates of the State Correctional Institution at Graterford. His second life, which began in June of that year, is the focus of the next several chapters.

The following material will give the reader a keen insight into the nature of imprisonment from a personal perspective. This, of course, cannot explain every detail of the phenomenon. Consider the old parable of the two blind men who encountered an elephant. Grabbing its leg, one exclaimed, "An elephant is like a tree!" Grabbing its tail, the other said, "No, an elephant is like a snake!" In this same sense, different readers will form different impressions of prison life after reading this narrative. All these impressions, however, will tap the same vein and, it is hoped, help them to better understand the experience of incarceration.

Introduction

In 1980, Iran was holding Americans hostage and Cuban refugees were flooding into Florida. Interest rates were at a record high, digital watches were the rage, and Jimmy Carter was president.

For me, Victor Hassine, the first half of 1980 was a very good year. I was in love and seriously considering marriage. I graduated from New York Law School in June and soon after left my internship with the Manhattan District Attorney to join a small law firm in my adopted hometown of Trenton, New Jersey. I had a brand-new sports car and a very promising future. Given that I had arrived in the United States 19 years earlier as a non-English speaking refugee escaping religious persecution in Egypt, I felt that I was the textbook example of a man who had achieved the American dream.

All that changed in November of 1980, when I was arrested in Pennsylvania and held without bail on charges of conspiring in a man's death. The state sought the death penalty. In June of 1981, despite my vigorous denial of the charges, a jury of my peers found me guilty of first-degree murder.

Immediately following the verdict, I was confined to a small holding cell in the basement of the Courthouse, while the jury deliberated for two days on whether to condemn me to death by electrocution or sentence me to life imprisonment without parole. They ultimately decided on the latter choice.

My odyssey through the Pennsylvania penal system began in June of 1981 with my arrival at the State Correctional Institution at Graterford (SCI-Graterford), an immense, walled facility lurking in the quiet countryside northwest of Philadelphia. I expected to find myself in a rigid, structured environment designed to deter and punish, even though I half hoped that inmates were being coddled as newspapers and TV reports had so often suggested. In any event, I assumed that everything was under control.

Within the first few weeks of incarceration, however, I began to realize that something was very wrong at Graterford. Fights were breaking out everywhere, the sale of drugs and contraband was commonplace, and it seemed as if everyone was carrying a weapon. Violence and corruption were rampant. Gangs ran the prison, terrorizing staff and inmates alike.

In my fourth month at Graterford, the prison was locked down while inmates with pistols and shotguns had a shootout with state police in a botched escape attempt that turned into a hostage situation. As the drama played itself out, I stayed in my cell for days, watching heavily armed state troopers rush back and forth.

In the months and years following the hostage crisis, prison life grew more violent, more uncontrolled, and a lot more crowded. I was in such a constant state of panic that I stopped feeling scared and just became desperate. I lived every moment as if it were my last, and I began to believe that I would never survive. I watched guards beating inmates and inmates beating and stabbing inmates and guards alike. I watched prison gangs rob and steal with impunity, while staff smuggled in contraband for sale on the black market. Rape was a common phenomenon of everyday life, as was sexual activity between inmates and staff members. There were no less than three riots in one 12-month period, all precipitated by electrical failures that caused blackouts on the housing blocks.

I had entered a system which seemed to exist only as a relentless generator of despair, corruption, and violence. I had become a "moment dweller" with no thoughts about the future. In my mind, I had imagined a greeting on the wall: *Welcome to Graterford Penitentiary. Abandon all hope ye who enter here.*

Chapter 1

How I Became a Convict

Editor's Note

Nature versus nurture is a hot topic of debate among criminologists. The idea of an innate or genetic "propensity to crime," which dates back to the early nineteenth-century positivist school, fell out of favor sometime after World War II. Whereas postwar criminologists were divided on the exact causes of criminal behavior, no thoughtful scholar espoused a theory of innate criminality. Likewise, postwar crime control programs focused on mechanisms that assume free will, particularly rehabilitation and deterrence. After 30 years, theories of innate criminality began to return in the 1970s. Today, criminologists are divided on the topic.

The author, whether or not he was born a criminal—if he is a criminal at all—was certainly not a convict when he arrived at Graterford in 1981. No one is born a convict. The innocent and guilty alike learn to "become" convicts. Success in prison depends on how fast and how well the new inmate learns. This process of "becoming" is a major area of sociological research.

I have heard Graterford called The Farm, The Camp, The Fort, and Dodge City, but I have never heard it called safe. When I was in the county jail awaiting trial, I saw grown men cry because their counselors told them they were being transferred to Graterford.

Graterford State Prison, Pennsylvania's largest and most violent penal institution, was built in the early 1930s to hold all of the state's most violent prisoners. On June 14, 1981, while it could not contain all 8,000 or more of the state's most wanted, it certainly had enough room to hold me. Its steel-reinforced concrete wall measures four feet thick by 32 feet tall and encloses over 65 acres of land. Originally designed to hold eight separate cell blocks within its perimeter, Graterford ended up with only five. But these cell blocks are huge constructions, each containing 400 cells.

Everything inside appears as huge and massive as the wall itself. Each housing unit is a rectangular structure, measuring about 45 feet wide by three stories tall by 820 feet long (over twice the length of a football field), perpendicularly attached to a quarter-mile-long main corridor which measures about 20 feet wide by two stories high.

I knew none of this as I sat handcuffed and shackled in the back seat of the sheriff's car, waiting to be taken inside to begin serving my life-without-parole sentence. All I could see was a blur of dirty, grainy whiteness from the giant wall that dominated the landscape before me. It made me feel very small and insignificant, and very frightened.

A giant steel gate rose up to allow the sheriff's car to drive into Graterford's cavernous sallyport area, a fortified enclosure designed to control traffic. Once the gate fell shut, I was immediately hustled out of the car by some very large, serious-looking corrections officers. I knew I would have to submit to a cavity search, but it wasn't the strip search that dominated my memory of this event. It was the *noise*.

Since concrete and steel do not absorb sound, the clamor and voices from within just bounced around, crashing into each other to create a hollow, booming echo that never ended. It sounded as if someone had put a microphone inside a crowded locker room with the volume pumped up, broadcasting the noise all around the sallyport. It was this deafening background noise that would lull me to sleep at night and greet me in the morning for the next five years. Though I have been out of Graterford for many years now, its constant din still echoes in my ears.

The prison guards finished their search and escorted me up Graterford's main corridor, a dim, gloomy, 20-foot-wide by over

1500-foot-long stretch. The lack of natural light and the damp, dungeon-like air in this place was oppressive. As I took one tentative step after another, I promised myself never to take bright and sunny places for granted again. Having just left the Courthouse hours before, I was so disoriented that I lost track of how far I had been walking.

Things changed with sudden permanence once I reached the central corridor gate that separated the administrative section from the prison proper. This was the first time I saw the faces, shapes, and shadows of the men who would become my future friends, enemies, and neighbors. They stared at me and I stared back, as scared as I had ever been in my entire life.

Once inside, I was walked through a gauntlet of desperate men. Their hot smell in the muggy corridor was as foul as their appearance. Most of them were wearing their "Graterford Tan," an ashen gray pallor. The discoloration of these distorted human forms represented the prison landscape. At Graterford you work, eat, sleep, and idle indoors. You never have to go outdoors unless you want to risk the sometimes deadly yard. Many inmates served their time like cave dwellers, never leaving Graterford's concrete and steel shelter.

My first impression was that most of these men brandished their scars and deformities like badges of honor. None of them seemed to have a full set of front teeth. Many bore prominently displayed tattoos of skulls or demons. They all seemed either too tall or too small, but none seemed right. Eyes were buggy, beady, squinted, or staring, but none were caring. Heads were too big, too small, pointed, swollen, or oblong, some with jutting foreheads, twisted noses, massive jaws, and gnarled hands. But none seemed human.

One could argue whether it was the look of these men that led them to prison or whether it was the prison that gave them their look. What tales of suffering their bodies told seemed to be of no concern to them. They were content to wear their scars openly like a warning, the way farmers use scarecrows to keep menacing birds away. Today I feel pity and compassion for those who have had to suffer so much pain and tragedy in one lifetime. But on that hot June day, all I wanted was to get away from these ugly creatures as quickly as possible. Just looking at them made me fear for my life. There was no pity or compassion in my heart then, because their grotesqueness made me forget they were human.

Now when I watch a new arrival walking "the gauntlet of desperate men," I can always sense his hopelessness. I know my staring is as horrifying to him as it was for me on my first day, and I know what I must look like to him.

Getting Classified

Toward the end of the main corridor I was shepherded into the shadowy expanse of yet another corridor. This led to the Clothing Room, a cold, damp place equipped with a tile-walled shower and an adjoining room where endless rows of mothballed clothes hung on racks like mismatched goods in a thrift shop.

My escort guard ordered me to "get naked" and surrender my personal effects to an inmate dressed in brown prison garb. I was still wearing my nice suit and tie from the Courthouse. As I stripped down, I handed the silent inmate the last vestiges of my social identity. He tossed them impatiently into an old cardboard box. After the guard conducted another "bend-over-and-stretch-'em" search, I was given delousing shampoo and ordered to shower.

As I stood naked and shivering after my shower, I was assigned two pairs of navy blue pants, two blue shirts, three T-shirts, three pairs of boxer shorts, three pairs of socks, a blue winter coat, a blue summer jacket, two towels, and a pair of brown shoes. Everything but the shoes and socks had "AM4737" boldly stamped in black. This number was my new, permanent identity.

Once I had dressed, I was taken to be fingerprinted and photographed, then escorted to E-Block, officially known as the Eastern Diagnostic and Classification Center (EDCC). Though Graterford had five cell blocks, only A- through D-Blocks were considered part of the prison. E-Block was treated as a separate facility, which inmates and staff called "Quarantine." Because all new receptions to Quarantine were issued blue prison uniforms, they were labeled "Blues." The general population inmates who wore brown uniforms were referred to as "Browns." Contact between Blues and Browns was strictly forbidden.

Soon I found myself before the E-Block Sergeant's desk, wearing my new blue uniform, cradling my belongings, and waiting for whatever came next. The Sergeant walked me to a room full of bedding. There another inmate in brown dropped a rolled-up mattress on my shoulder. Inside it were stuffed a blanket, pillow, metal cup, plastic knife, fork, and spoon, a pack of rolling tobacco, soap, toothbrush, toothpaste, and a disposable razor.

Awkwardly balancing the mattress roll on my shoulder with one arm and carrying my prison-issued clothes with the other, I followed the Sergeant down a flight of stairs to my cell on one of the bottom ranges. The moment I twisted my body and cargo sideways into the dark, narrow cell, the Sergeant slid the door shut and disappeared from sight.

The next two days were spent in the prison's infirmary for shots and a complete medical examination. While it was a doctor who examined me, it was an inmate who drew my blood and wrote down my medical history. Since the infirmary was also used by Browns from general population, a guard followed me and the other receptions everywhere we went. This constant surveillance had me wondering why we were so heavily guarded.

I later learned that any exposure of Browns to Blues was closely watched by the staff. One reason was that, since they had more liberties than the new arrivals, Browns often tried to barter privileges with Blues. For example, a pack of cigarettes could buy extra phone time or a library pass; and for a pack a day, you could rent a TV or a radio. Also, some Browns were homosexuals and would exploit weaker Blues. Almost all of them were point men for prison gangs, who reported back on the new prospects among Blues for possible gang membership or future victimization.

After I completed the medical examination process, there were about two weeks of idleness. Finally I was taken to an Examination Room on the block for a series of written psychological and literacy tests. There was no supervision in this room, and the testing process took about two days.

Two months of more idleness followed as I waited to be interviewed by my counselor. There were over 400 inmates on E-Block and many fights. It seemed as if every time the block was let out into the yard, a fight would break out somewhere. From my experience, when convicts are let loose after being locked up for long periods of time, aggressive behavior is an immediate and natural consequence.

To occupy time, people played cards and worked out. It was during these idle days in classification that longstanding friendships and alliances were made and when inmates distinguished the weak from the strong—predators from victims.

The first impressions I made on others during classification have stayed with me in prison ever since. Since I was not a career criminal, I was initially viewed as a "square john": a middle-class outsider with no experience of the social world of inmates. To both my advantage and disadvantage, I was seeing everything through the eyes of a foreigner, making many foolish mistakes yet gaining just as many unique insights into their world.

When I was finally called in for my interview, the counselor examined my test results and asked me a minimum of questions about my conviction and sentence. The interview took only ten to 15 minutes.

Two weeks later, I was summoned to appear before the Classification Committee. Sitting before a counselor, the block Sergeant, and a Major of the Guards, I was asked what prison I wanted to go to and why. I could only suggest Graterford since I didn't think other prisons would be any better or worse. Then I waited outside while they reviewed my file. Within a few minutes, I was called back and informed that I had been classified to Graterford. Just before I left, the Major added in a pleasant voice, "You'll be working for me."

At the time I didn't consider the significance of my job assignment. I was too relieved to know that the tortuous classification ordeal was finally over. A few days later, I traded in my blues for browns and moved off Quarantine into the general population.

To me and most of the others, as I later discovered, classification was a total waste of time. While different prisons in Pennsylvania purportedly provided different types of rehabilitation programs meant to serve the needs of various kinds of offenders, in reality it seemed that only three considerations were used to determine a convict's ultimate destination: (1) race, (2) hometown, and (3) availability of cell space. At the time, most of the minority inmates in the state were classified to Graterford or Western Penitentiary. The other seven prisons consisted of mostly white inmates under an all-white civilian staff.

From the inmate point of view, the testing was an utter sham. For one thing, the written tests were given to everyone without even determining who could read or write. The written tests I took were in an unsupervised room with about 30 other men, most of whom just picked answers at random or copied them from someone else.

Because the tests were given so irrelevantly, inmates tended to see their results only as a tool of manipulation. Under this assumption, many men had developed theories on how to answer the test questions. Some felt it was best to copy from the brightest men in order to improve their chances at getting a clerk's job over kitchen or laundry duty. Others felt they should give lunatic answers so they could be medically released from work altogether. Still others gave no answers at all and faked illiteracy. Such men reasoned that they could enroll in school and appear to do extremely well, thereby fooling the parole board into believing they had worked hard to make a positive change in their lives. All these connivances were based on the inmates' understanding that they were being conned as much as they were doing the conning.

Getting Dug In

Inmates serving long sentences preferred to lock at Graterford because, even though it was violent, it afforded them the most personal liberty. This was so because the more violent a prison is, the more reluctant guards are to enforce petty rules for fear of being assaulted.

Once I was classified to Graterford, I had to move my belongings, along with my mattress, blanket, and pillow, to B-Block. This was a working block, reserved only for those inmates who had been assigned a job. My assignment turned out to be a fortuitous clerical job in the Major of the Guards' office. All my belongings were fit into a single shopping bag which I carried in one hand, while my rolled-up mattress was once again toted on my shoulder. I walked down the long main corridor to B-Block, my new home. Though it mirrored the design of E-Block, it was considerably less crowded and noisy. Comparatively, this hell seemed more like heaven to me.

The first thing I noticed was that the men on B-Block were much older than most of those on the classification block. These were the "Old Heads" of the prison, inmates who had done a long stretch. When I arrived at my assigned cell, I quickly signed in at the Block Sergeant's desk and requested cleaning supplies. Then I spent the morning scrubbing down every inch of my cell. By noon count I was able to lie down on my bed, smoke a cigarette, and consider what I was going to do next.

My cell measured about six feet by 12 with a ten-foot high ceiling, from which dangled a single light bulb with a drawstring switch. For furniture, I had a flat, hard steel bed and a steel desk and chair which had been assembled as one unit. The mandatory toilet afforded a sink directly above it with a steel medicine cabinet above that. High over the toilet was a rusty radiator which served as my only source of heat in the winter. Finally, I had a flimsy wooden foot locker with a hasp that could be locked with a commissary-bought combination lock.

My cell entrance was a solid steel sliding door with a fixed glass window on the top quarter. On the opposite wall was a window that could be manually opened and closed, just a little. The concrete walls were painted a dingy off-white and adorned with graffiti and cigarette stains.

Despite the grim accommodations, this was my home. I was due to report to work the next morning and I could feel myself getting dug in. In prison it doesn't take much to make a man happy: food, some quiet, a good book, a job, and enough heat in the winter. That day I was happy just to be able to lie on that hard bed with a 70-watt light bulb glaring in my face. I felt the worst was over. I could now begin to serve my time.

Escape From Reality

Like most first-time arrivals to Graterford, I was only preoccupied with survival and how to avoid becoming the victim of violence. This sudden refocusing of attention led me to change my habits, my personality, and even my values. With these changes came a new way of viewing the world as a place of unrelenting fear.

If I made eye contact with a stranger, I would feel threatened. An unexpected smile could mean trouble. A man in uniform was not a friend. Being kind was a weakness. Viciousness and recklessness were to be respected and admired. Oddly enough, these changes were in some way comforting. In the struggle to survive, it was easier to distrust everyone than to believe in their inherent goodness.

Danger became a determining factor of the changes in my attitude and personality. When there was general movement in the prison, for example, the main corridor would fill with hundreds of inmates in transit. This made the corridor an extremely dangerous place to be. I was more likely to see a stabbing than a guard on duty.

The cell blocks were just as insecure. A guard at one end of a cell block could not identify anyone at the other end; the distance of 700 feet was just too great. Because of their fear of being assaulted where no one could see them, many block guards never patrolled the inner perimeter and spent most of their time avoiding conflicts at all cost, even turning the other way.

By the time I had settled in, however, I found myself feeling safe enough to think beyond the moment. This was something I had not been able to do since my arrest. Unfortunately, this new sense of security brought with it the "sleeping phase." I began to sleep 12 to 14 hours a day. My whole life consisted of eating, working, and sleeping. I never dreamed. I only tried to stay unconscious for as long as I possibly could.

Though I had no way of knowing it at the time, I had entered a very common prison-adjustment phase. So common, in fact, that walking in on a newcomer while he sleeps is the most practiced technique of cell thieves and rapists. In Graterford, a man who spends too much time in bed sends the same signal as that of a bleeding fish in shark-infested waters.

"You can't be sleeping all the time," cautioned my chess partner one day, waking me to play a game. "You can't sleep away your sentence. You have to stay awake to stay alive in here."

He was right, and I knew it. So I resolved to keep myself busy. I took up reading and painting as hobbies. I was allowed to buy almost as many books, magazines, and newspapers as I wanted, as well as canvasses, brushes, and paints. Self-help was encouraged so long as you could pay for it yourself.

Soon I was reading everything I could get my hands on and painting well into the wee hours of the morning. My cell became crowded with books, magazines, canvasses, newspapers, and even an easel. I went so far as to rig up extra lighting, hang pictures, and buy throw rugs for the cement floor. I had successfully transformed my cell into a cluttered boarding-house room.

Like some literary critic and master artist, I was so deeply submerged in my hobbies that I became as obsessed as a man digging his way to freedom. But I was no literary critic and certainly no artist. I was just another lifer trying to escape the real world.

"You have to spend more time out of that cell, Victor," insisted my chess mate and only friend at that time. "It's not healthy to do a 'bit' [time] like that. Look at your cell, you have junk everywhere. You even have lights on your wall that look like they belong in a room somewhere else."

"I'm just getting dug in," I replied in defense, annoyed that my efforts at avoiding reality had been detected.

"This isn't getting dug in, this is foolishness. You're in a penitentiary—a tough one. You should never try to forget that. Never try to make yourself believe you're somewhere else. Do you know what a lit match could do to this cell?"

His words struck an unnerving chord. Only a few months earlier, I had watched a man whose cell across the way had been deliberately set on fire. He had screamed and banged helplessly on his locked door, flames dancing around him, biting at his flesh. Through his cell window, I could see billowing black smoke envelope his pleading, twisted, horrfied face until he disappeared. It had taken some time before guards responded to his screams.

The very next day I gave away my books, magazines, newspapers, art supplies, and my easel. I knew I had to fight as hard for my safety as I did for my sanity.

Prison Slang

As a child immigrant who neither spoke nor understood English, I once had to face the strange, intimidating world of the American school system. But I overcame my fear of the unfamiliar because of my strong desire to adapt to a community of classmates. I wanted desperately to belong and to speak their language.

Likewise, from the outset of my term in Graterford I once again found myself in a frightening world where I couldn't understand the language or the behavior of its inhabitants. But I felt that same desperate urge to belong to a community of inmates in the strange, new world of the American penal system. Everyone in prison—staff and inmates alike—seemed to know each other not only personally but intimately. They laughed and interacted like siblings, even during exchanges of anger. This strong familiarity gave the population of Graterford the appearance of one big clan. I wanted to be accepted by this clan, to know its secrets, and to speak its language.

One of the first things I knew I had to do was to adapt myself to the pervasive use of jailhouse slang by both inmates and staff. The tenor of this prison lingo was generally vulgar and aggressive, expressed with self-important arrogance. Yet at the same time it exhibited an unbridled honesty that implied a certain unconditional tolerance for the opinions and beliefs of others.

The first column below provides a typical monologue of current prison slang, one that might be heard on any given day in Graterford. The second column is the non-slang English version. This is a just a brief sample from the vast repertoire of expressions used in the prison population today.

Graterford Version	*English Version*
Three homeys played a tip and did a B & E on the humbug. Dudes were stick-up boys, not back-door boosters, so they weren't down with it. Turns out to be a fat take. They find the stash and it's full of gold, rocks, paper, and cash money.	Three neighborhood friends followed up on a tipster's information and committed a house burglary on a sudden impulse. These men were armed robbers and not burglars so they were not familiar with the business. As it turned out, they stole a lot of money. They found a cache full of gold, precious stones, negotiable instruments, and cash.
After breaking down the tip man, the cutees get to breaking down the gapper, when one of the homeys throws shit into the game and pulls out a gat, talking about, "I ain't breaking down with no lames." He plucks one dude and goes to capping the other, but ain't nothing slow about home boy and he breaks camp.	After the man who tipped them off about the house was paid off, the three partners began to divide the money. One of them complicated matters by pulling a gun, saying, "I'm not sharing any money with losers." He killed one cohort, but the other one was faster and managed to get away.
Now cutee's fast but he's a trembler, he ain't got no ticker for this kind of drama. He gets to dry snitching to the police, talking	While the man who escaped was fast, he was frightened and didn't have the courage to deal with this kind of situation. He went to

about, "Officer, I heard some shooting at so and so, I think such and such might know something about it." Police bust the dude with the gapper and the gat. He ends up taking 12 in the box but pulls a life sentence with a nickel to a dime running wild.

Dude caught a bad break on a good score. If he'd broke down with his homeys, instead of pulling that slimy shit, he'd be living large.

the police and hinted about the shooter's acts by saying, "Officer, I heard some shooting at such and such a place and so and so might know something about it." The police ended up arresting the shooter with the money and the gun. He took a jury trial but was found guilty and received a life sentence with a five-to-ten-year sentence running consecutive to the life sentence.

The guy caught a bad break. If he had shared the money with his friends, instead of being underhanded, he would be living a very rich life.

Chapter 2

Things Missed

Editor's Note

"Punishment" is a central theme of the prison experience and, not surprisingly, a constant topic of debate. At the most abstract level, criminologists often argue whether punishment serves higher-level social functions. Does punishment reinforce social bonds, for example, as Durkheim argued? At a more pragmatic level, criminologists debate the effectiveness of punishment. Does punishment deter criminal behavior, for example, either by the person being punished (specific deterrence) or in others (general deterrence)? Within this debate, it is important to remember that the first American prisons, built in the late eighteenth century, were designed to replace punishments that were deemed inhumane—whipping, maiming, and hanging. When punishments were used in early American prisons, moreover, they were explicit and independent of imprisonment. The "punishments" that the author describes in this chapter, on the other hand, are implicit; that is, they are part and parcel of the prison experience. Readers may wonder whether the implicit punishments are any better or worse than the explicit punishments that prisons were designed to replace.

Punishments for Misconduct

Reprimand and Warning

A warning from the Hearing Examiner not to do it again, "or else!"

Loss of Privileges

Suspension of privileges for a given period of time. These privileges include visiting, phone calls, commissary, yard, work, and television.

Cell Restriction

Confinement to one's cell except for meal lines and two hours per day recreation on the block, and loss of job. All other privileges are left intact unless specifically suspended.

Double-lock Feed-in

Confined to one's cell except for two hours recreation on the block and three showers per week. Loss of job, all privileges suspended or curtailed, and three full meals in the cell.

Disciplinary Custody

The Hole, or "Siberia." Solitary confinement in the isolation unit (Restrictive Housing Unit, or RHU) with all privileges suspended or curtailed. Three full meals in the RHU cell, and two hours recreation per day.

One of the more subtle ways a prison punishes is by its neglect of a man's need for things, both the abstract (e.g., his freedom) and the tangible (e.g., his personal property). From the very start, I began missing both. Just when I would get accustomed to doing without old things, I would start to miss new things. It was almost as if prison life had created a newfound desire in me to miss something all the time.

At first, I missed the obvious: sex, love, family, and friends. But it wasn't long before I stopped missing these things and started focusing on the next wave of things I no longer have: privacy, quiet, and peace of mind, intangibles that I have never stopped missing to this day.

There are no trees in the great walled fortress of Graterford and very few shrubs. In fact, there isn't much of anything green that hasn't been painted that color. Also, the prison is designed so that you can never get an unobstructed view of anything. Walls keep getting in the way.

Occasionally when I had to make trips outside the prison for court appearances or doctor visits, I would sit in the prison van enraptured by the trees whizzing past. The brightness and the beautiful colors of everything around me made every outside trip an exciting experience. I know of several men who filed lawsuits or feigned illnesses just to get "some streets."

Well aware of this, the administration would try to make such trips as uncomfortable as possible. They would handcuff and shackle traveling inmates and strip-search every man coming and going, even though he never left the sight of an officer. They would make certain that an inmate wore ill-fitting clothes that were dirty, torn, and extremely uncomfortable. In the winter they had only summer clothes available and only winter garments in the summer. For a while they even required a man to be locked in his cell the day before making such a trip.

But no amount of discouragement worked. Inmates loved these trips, because they reminded them of all the things they missed. Personally, I always came back from each trip dwelling on the trees, the beautiful women, and all the joys of the outside world I was deprived of. Longing for these things made me take a lot of risks in my efforts to reclaim even the most insignificant of things that I once had taken for granted.

Having It My Way

My first misconduct at Graterford resulted from missing one of life's simplest pleasures: a fresh-cooked burger. I had just come out of classification and started working the 12-to-8 p.m. shift as a clerk in the Major of the Guards' office, which was off the main corridor between E and D Block. One day a contraband sandwich merchant, or "swag man," walked into the office and offered me a ten-pound bag of frozen ground beef for a pack of cigarettes. I had no way of cooking it, but for another pack I could get a hot plate. I began to imagine myself biting into a hot, juicy hamburger sandwich grilled to my liking. I bought the contraband beef, which was a bargain considering that a pack of cigarettes at that time cost only 50 cents in the commissary.

A senior clerk helped me out by talking to an inmate kitchen worker, who quickly produced the heating element of an electric coffee urn and an aluminum cookie pan, both hidden in the lining of his oversized prison-issued coat. For only one more cigarette pack, he scrounged up hamburger buns, chopped onions, butter, sliced cheese, ketchup, mustard, and two bricks to hold the cookie pan over the heating element.

That evening when the meat had finally thawed, my co-conspirators and I set up a makeshift grill in the Major's bathroom. We fashioned burger patties and started frying the hamburgers as soon as movement in the main corridor had ended.

It was the onions that did us in. The aroma of sauted onions in butter was so strong that it attracted a guard stationed some 300 feet away. He followed the aroma to its origin and asked us for a burger. We were more than happy to share with him, and he was eating it as he left the office, which made us all sigh with relief.

A few minutes later, a Search Team raided us and confiscated everything. They had been tipped off when the previous guard offered one of them a bite of his tasty burger. When they asked him where he had gotten it, he simply told them. Apparently the members of the Search Team were not as impressed with our resourcefulness.

In the early 1980s, Graterford introduced the Search Team, or "A Team," as a special two-man guard squad whose sole function was to conduct cell searches and pat downs. Not even the block officers knew who or when they would strike. Whenever a Search Team entered a block, an inmate would call out, "Search Team up!" Inmates at the end of the block would immediately hide their contraband. Because it took so long for the team to make it down the long block, contraband was able to be moved constantly without detection.

Given that our hamburger caper took place in the Major's office, however, we didn't have that advantage. We were all issued misconduct reports for the possession of contraband. Following a misconduct hearing, I was found guilty, removed from my job, and forced to pay for the food. I was also confined to my cell for 60 days, allowed out only two hours per day for recreation on the block. As shown at the beginning of this chapter, "cell restriction" is classified as a third-level punishment for misconduct.

My biggest mistake in this case was my naiveté. Until the Search Team had confiscated the burgers, I thought that such activity was merely business as usual at Graterford. I had only been in general population for about a month, and things developed with such effortless ease that I hadn't taken what I had done very seriously. For many years afterward, my prison handle became "Burger King," even though I had never gotten a chance to taste the object of my crime.

The Hole

Every prison attempts to gain a specific end in some way, be it deterrence, punishment, and/or rehabilitation. What makes a prison unnatural is the way it tries to achieve that end. For example, a prison imposes communal existence on people who would normally segregate themselves from society or from each other, such as blacks and whites. And, despite the endless promulgation of rules, their enforcement is so arbitrary that inmates live in a constant state of uncertainty.

Disciplinary segregation, or the "Hole," serves no ultimate end but to deprive a man of *all* things except the bare necessities of survival. It is a highly contradictory experience for every inmate. To some it is punishment, to others it is safety, and to still others it is just another way to do time. Furthermore, solitary confinemnent is completely contrary to a prison's principle of imposed communal living.

From my own experiences in the Hole, the only thing that saved me from falling into the great abyss that separates the sane from the insane was the fact that I could read. For the illiterate, solitary confinement is a one-way ticket to madness.

While I was in the Hole, I discovered illiterate inmates who managed to alter their mental states enough to make the Hole their home, even convincing themselves that they preferred the "independence" of the Hole. Generally, they adapted to their environment in one of two ways: they totally threw themselves at the mercy of the guards in order to satisfy their hunger for conversation, or they communicated with other Hole residents by shouting from cell to cell for hours at a time. As I spent my time reading, I could hear their loud chatter as they tried to hang onto some last vestige of sanity.

One important thing that the Hole made me realize was how essential education should be to a prison system. I came to this conclusion because it seemed that only a literate inmate can truly know and understand the punishment attached to his wrongful acts.

At one point I had an opportunity to talk with an illiterate young man in the cell next to mine. He was doing disciplinary time for fighting. During most of his waking hours, he would sit on the floor next to the bars of his cell and talk to me or anyone else about everything and nothing. I knew he could not read so I understood what he was doing and tolerated his constant intrusion into my solitary world of reading.

One day he asked me what day it was and how many more days he had to go. The first thing I always did in the Hole was to keep some kind of a calendar, lest they forget to let me out on time. After some quick math, I told him he had only 28 days left. He then asked when that would be. I didn't understand the question, until he explained that he wanted to know how many more Sundays he would have to do.

This young man's illiteracy was so profound that he had no concept of time. To him the number 28 was as remote as the number 1,000,000. So if he didn't understand the length of his disciplinary time, there was no way he could fully comprehend the time the courts had given him to serve his sentence in prison.

If a man's illiteracy prevented him from understanding relative lengths of time, then what other things couldn't he understand? How could he ever possibly be deterred if he can only fathom the consequences of his actions *after* he has experienced them? Literacy should be high on the critical list of missed things for such a man, especially if he doesn't even know what he's missing.

After my conversation with my young Hole neighbor, I didn't give it much more thought. I immersed myself back into my book, but only after I checked my pencil-marked calendar and thanked God for the few remaining days I had left. I also thanked God for allowing me to be literate enough to understand time, space, and the Hole.

The Inmate's Dilemma

The foremost tangible things missed by an inmate are his stolen personal possessions, particularly the few things he can keep in his cell. Graterford's neglect of the right to property was an insidious one because of its widespread epidemic of cell thefts.

Fortunately for me, everybody on B-Block where I lived had jobs. This meant that most of them made enough money to shop at the commissary every week. Some of them had manufacturing jobs in Correctional Industries, such as weaving, shoemaking, or tailoring, and could make well over a 100 dollars a month if they worked overtime. By prison standards this was considered to be a small fortune.

Total employment meant that there was not a major theft problem on B-Block at the time. This was a great relief to me, not because I didn't expect to get some of my things stolen, but because I didn't want to deal with the inevitability of catching some thief in the act.

In the life of an inmate, if you catch someone stealing from you, you're compelled to deal with it physically. This is not because you want to or you think it's the right thing to do, but because you absolutely must. If someone steals from you and you decide to report him to the guards, all that will happen is that the thief will go to the Hole for a while. Soon he'll be back in population and ready to seek revenge. Revenge in prison can take place years after its initiation. It generally occurs when you are vulnerable and the avenger happens to be around. This reality will leave you constantly looking over your shoulder. Additionally, involving the guards will get you the reputation as a "snitch," which means you will be physically challenged by inmates seeking to make a reputation or pass their own "snitch" label onto you.

If you choose to ignore the theft, the man will steal from you again and tell his friends, who in turn will also steal from you. Eventually, you will be challenged for more than just minor belongings. This "Inmate's Dilemma" is precisely why most men in prison hope they never have to deal with a sloppy cell thief. Unfortunately, many men who were caught stealing on the streets will just as easily get caught stealing in prison.

By 1982, there was no way an inmate could lock his own cell at Graterford. Cells were all locked or opened simultaneously at given intervals by the pulling of a single lever. At 6:00 a.m., for example, all the cells on the block were levered open so each inmate could open and close his own cell during breakfast. Five minutes after last call for breakfast, the levers were pulled again to lock all the doors. If you returned late from breakfast, you would have to wait for all the cells to be levered open again before you could re-enter your cell. In case of an emergency, each guard had a key which could override the lever and let you in. But asking a guard to key you in was like asking for a key out of the prison.

This process of opening and closing all doors at once was repeated at 8:00 a.m. for work lines and yard line; then again at 11:00 a.m. for count; at noon for lunch; at 5:00 p.m. for count; at 6:00 p.m. for supper; at 6:30 p.m. for block out, yard out, or work lines; then finally at 9:00 p.m. for final count and lockdown. Every one of us religiously followed this schedule because we always wanted to be at our cells when they opened up. Otherwise, we stood the chance of losing everything of value.

To combat theft, I arranged a neighborhood-watch system with my neighbors to look out for my cell when I wasn't there and vice versa. But for the most part it was every man for himself. From time to time I would return to my cell and discover things missing.

Fortunately I have never had to face the Inmate's Dilemma, but many others have and the consequences were brutal. There is no walking away in Graterford—the walls see to that—so either the intruder or the victim ends up seriously hurt.

One example of a cell confrontation involved not a cell thief but a Peeping Tom. One of my cell-block neighbors was Dip, a cocky body builder with an imposing physique. He was convinced that the mere sight of his impressive frame would deter anyone from ever messing with him. While other inmates ran to their cells when the levers were thrown to protect their belongings, Dip never bothered.

Then one day Dip returned to his cell from a shower, wearing only a towel around his nakedness. To his shock, he found an inmate hiding under his bed with an exposed erection, trying to watch him undress. Dip was so caught off guard that the intruder simply walked out, blowing him a kiss as he turned to run off the block. Once he had recovered his senses, Dip got very mad. He dressed himself for combat and stormed down the block to find the man who had challenged his manhood. The jeers and heckles of neighboring inmates only served to deepen his rage.

But the moment Dip stepped into the main corridor, the kiss blower was waiting with some friends. Dip was stabbed several times with homemade knifes. Lucky for him, his injuries were only "Graterford wounds," meaning that his vital parts were still intact. By the time guards had made it to the scene, the attackers were gone,

one of their knives was left behind, and bleeding Dip was locked up—charged with possession of the weapon that had been used to stab him.

For the most part, the prison administration did nothing to curb cell thefts or invasion of cell privacy. Some guards also seemed to think that these thefts and intrusions were part of the punishment attached to doing time. In due time, however, the administration's failure to provide adequate safety and security would have far-reaching consequences.

Throughout 1981 and 1982, inmates petitioned, begged, and even threatened in their efforts to convince the administration to provide some means by which inmates could lock their own cells. The administration rejected these requests, claiming that cells were secure enough. If the administration had conceded to such requests, it would have been a tacit admission that they did not have control over their own prison.

By 1982, Graterford's general population rose to over 2,000. Every cell in the general population blocks was occupied and in the classification block the new receptions were already being double-celled. There were not enough jobs to go around now, so many men sat idle on B-Block. This resulted in more theft, which in turn led to more fights and more stabbings.

The Day of Locking Cells

As thievery increased, gangs flourished. Some gangs were formed to steal, others to defend against burglaries and robberies. Since B-Block was comprised mostly of working inmates, the fighting was not as frequent. But D and C Blocks were virtual war zones. There were so many fights and retaliations that guards were getting injured in the melees.

Only then did the administration take action. Holes were drilled in the cell-door tracks so that any cell could be locked from the outside with a padlock, even when the master lever was opened. The commissary began selling padlocks that could fit in the hole. There was a general feeling of relief, because we could now secure our belongings. It seemed less likely now that we would ever have to deal with the Inmate's Dilemma—or so we thought.

Once gangs form in a prison, they're hard to break up. When a group of cell thieves join together, no lock can stop them. Their incentive had increased now as well, especially since this new sense of security encouraged inmates to keep a lot more valuable goods in their cells.

To get around the new cell locks, thieves simply changed their techniques. The problem that remained was that when the master lever was open and the inmate was inside his cell, he could not lock himself inside the cell. Instead of waiting until an inmate left his cell, a gang would simply rush into the cell while he was sleeping or using the commode. This resulted in even more fights and stabbings. Burglary is one thing, but strong-armed robbery demands an immediate and violent response. As the number of robberies and assaults surged, the new jailhouse wisdom was that you should always be awake and ready to fight when cells were opened, and that you should use the commode only when your cell was locked.

Some prisoners began fashioning weapons that could withstand a shakedown. For example, they would keep wooden floor brushes in their cells. Made of solid oak, these heavy brushes could render a man unconscious. Since they were prison issue, they weren't considered contraband. If a guard found one in your cell, all he could do was confiscate it or order you to return it to the Block Sergeant. Ironically, the heavy-duty combination locks sold in the commissary served as another shakedown-proof weapon. Placed in a sock, this weapon could be more effective than most homemade knives.

The ultimate defense against unwanted intruders was getting a hole drilled on the *inside* of your door. A bolt secured in this hole prevented the door from being opened, so you could now lock your cell from the inside as well as from the outside. The staff objected to this hole on the grounds that an inmate could barricade himself in his cell so it could only be opened with a cutting torch. If a guard saw a hole on the inside of your door, he might plug it up with metal solder, but it was easy enough to get another hole drilled.

A combination lock on the inside door-jamb hole rendered a man's cell fairly secure. The ability to keep more property without being restricted to their cells freed inmates from the routine of protecting their belongings. This meant more socialization, recreation, and work. It also meant the gangs would have to change their style of doing business once again. The treasures now accumulating in the cells were just too much to resist.

Chapter 3

Prison Violence

Editor's Note

Like most modern prisons, Graterford is a violent institution. Although historical data are unavailable, criminologists believe this trend of increasing violence a recent phenomenon. Its causes are unknown. Some attribute the increase in prison violence to overcrowding per se, though the evidence may not be enough to substantiate this. When American prisons became overcrowded after the end of World War II, for example, the level of violence did not seem to rise in the affected institutions. Other criminologists attribute the trend to one or more specific inadequacies of prisons, ranging from a lack of psychological programs and services to permissive administrators. Finally, like Victor Hassine, there are those who point to changes in the larger society. Prisons have grown more violent, they argue, because society has grown more violent.

This "cultural importation" hypothesis is interesting in its simplicity, yet it tends to exonerate prison administrators from any blame. Some years ago, Governor Lester Maddox explained the deplorable condition of his state's prisons in this way: "I'll give you better prisons when you give me better prisoners."

As a scientific theory, the thesis of cultural importation can be problematic. Apparent exceptions are seen whenever there is a radical change in the prison-bound population. As the imprisonment of the mentally ill became more common, for example, the prevalence of anti-psychotic medications in prisons rose. The sudden appearance of AIDS is another example. (Hassine discusses both phenomena in later chapters.) Examples of the importation of cultural norms, however, are less common.

Rumor had it that Old Man Simpson had been beaten by the KKK as a young man and by white guards in prison. If you were white and walked within arms' reach of him, Old Man Simpson would punch you in the face without warning. He also had a habit of throwing piping hot coffee in any white man's face who stood too close to him in the breakfast line. Prison veterans always steered clear of him and enjoyed watching him do his thing to the newcomers.

But Old Man Simpson's acts of violence were mild compared to such random acts of savagery as those of the young inmates who swept through the crowded main corridor and threw concentrated cleaning acid into men's faces, or the prison gang who stormed a cell block and slashed inmates' necks and faces with razor blades.

By 1984, Graterford's population exceeded 2,500. Gangs proliferated at a staggering rate, not only because of high unemployment but because of the need for protection from the gangs' new money-making schemes.

If you couldn't rob a man's cell, you just robbed the man himself. Extortion became very lucrative. One of the favorite ways to deal with a resistant victim was to lock him in his cell and set the cell on fire. So if you were not aligned with a protection gang, it was only a matter of time before you would have to face the "Welcome Wagon" and be forced to pay or fight.

These were violent and deadly times at Graterford; times of random violence, murders, cell fires, paranoia, and knife carrying. According to the Department of Corrections' Monthly Morbidity Report in 1986-87, Graterford accounted for the highest rate of assaults out of Pennsylvania's 12 state prisons: 392 assaults by inmates against inmates and 47 by inmates against staff, a total of 439.

While it seemed like total anarchy, it really wasn't. This was mob rule with a purpose, a throwback to a time long before civilized man developed modern social institutions. By now I began to realize how fragile civilization was and how easily modern man could be reduced to the savagery of his prehistoric ancestors. Though we had

TVs, radios, clothes, and a wealth of commissary goods, behaviorally we had regressed thousands of years backward on the social evolutionary scale. The new order was now the law of the jungle.

Violence in Graterford had also become a form of escape for many inmates. In creating and maintaining a predatory environment, these men were able to avoid the reality of imprisonment by focusing all their attention on fighting one another. The more hostile the environment, the more they saw themselves as victims and the less responsible they felt for their own actions. This obsession with violence became as destructive as any narcotic addiction.

People caught up in this violent escapism never perceived it as their reaction to incarceration, any more than I could see the danger of oversleeping. Sadly, the ones who ended up suffering the most were those who came to prison just to pay their debt to society— those who hoped one day to return to their lives in the mainstream. They suffered twice: once at the hands of the predatory inmates, and then again through the prison's system of punishment.

Prison Subcultures

One of the contributing factors to this upsurge of violence was the creation of new subcultures within the prison. These arose from the new types of inmates who had now extended the roster of victims and predators in the general population. People who in the past would never have been committed to an adult correction facility were now queuing up for their "three hots and a cot" in ever-increasing numbers.

Many of these were the mentally ill who had spilled out of state mental hospitals, which had been closed down in the seventies. These "nuts," as inmates simply called them, were pathetic and destructive. Their illnesses made punishment in the normal sense virtually impossible. Their helplessness often made them the favorite victims of predatory inmates. Worst of all, their special needs and peculiar behavior destroyed the stability of the prison system.

There were also growing numbers of the homeless, as well as juvenile offenders committed as adults. But the largest group of new arrivals were young, minority drug dealers and users, most of them from inner-city ghettos.

When the homeless came to Graterford, they were just looking for a secure haven from the streets. They weren't interested in counselors, treatment, or discipline. They had no sense of their own criminality.

Juveniles suffered the most. They viewed prison as a surrogate parent and so expected to be protected and sheltered. What they got instead was victimization by adult inmates and indifferent bureaucrats.

Finally, the drug addicts and dealers saw Graterford as one more rehab center to dry them up and help them overcome their habit. Few thought of themselves as criminals because they perceived themselves as the victims of their own addictions.

Like me, all these newcomers sought to have their needs met. But Graterford, a maximum-security prison, could not identify these needs, let alone meet them. A prison confines, punishes, and hopefully deters. It is neither designed nor inclined to foster, cure, or rehabilitate.

In meeting only the basic needs of the new arrivals (food, shelter, clothing, and medical care), Graterford's resources were stretched beyond its limits. Additionally, many of the guards and treatment staff, who were accustomed to supplying inmates with only a minimum amount of services and a maximum amount of discipline, were embittered by the fact that these new arrivals were coming into the prison with expectations of receiving treatment and care.

Soon, the mentally ill were commanding too much of the staff's attention. Drug addicts, many of them going through withdrawal, were doing anything they could to get high. Juveniles were being raped and causing havoc trying to attract some "parental" attention. Because of all this, instead of changing people, Graterford itself was changing. Since most of the new commitments came from blighted urban areas, the changes often reflected that environment.

New Inmates vs. Old Heads

Fear and violence had changed Graterford as profoundly as it had changed me. The new prison subcultures with their disrespect for authority, drug addiction, illiteracy, and welfare mentality had altered the institution's very character. All the evils of the decaying American inner city were being compressed into one overcrowded prison. Ironically, the violence which had long been a tool of control by the administration was now being used against it to send its prison system hurtling out of control. Much of the violence that invaded Graterford in the 1980s was actually imported from the streets by the social misfits who were now being called convicts. They were criminals before—the only change in their identity is that now they're incarcerated. For many of these newcomers, prison violence was simply life as usual.

Reacting to this new environment, the Old Heads would tell anyone who would listen about the "good old days." The typical Old Head had come to Graterford a decade or more earlier after spending most of his life behind bars. What puzzled me and others my age was how these seasoned prison elders would pine over the rigidly structured routine, solitude, mistreatment, and hard labor of those good old days. When asked about it, they would talk about times when the outside world was kept outside, when an inmate's natural enemies were the guards, and when men did extraordinary things to go home.

Now those good old days had become a bygone era. To the Old Heads, prison life today lacked the honor, quiet solitude, and routine that had once made incarceration more noble. Now the greatest threat to an inmate had become other inmates, particularly the "young bucks" who had infested the general population.

An example of this new threat was the way debts were collected. Old Heads were always careful to whom they gave credit. If a debtor fell behind in payments, the debt was usually doubled and any of his belongings would be taken as collateral. Physical violence was employed only as a last resort.

In contrast, the young bucks would lend anything to anybody. Should a debtor be late in paying, even if it was a single pack of cigarettes, he would immediately be beaten and robbed. It seemed almost as if these compulsive youths were more interested in committing violence than in making money. This all too common practice of swift punishment for indebtedness disturbed the Old Heads' sense of fair play. "Working from the muscle" was to them unsound business, but the young bucks would have it no other way. To the Old Heads nothing in business was personal, but to the young newcomers *everything* was personal.

What disturbed the Old Heads most was how these newcomers had so readily and completely accepted prison as their life. Everything they did, including using and dealing drugs, smuggling contraband, forming violent gangs, and embracing homosexuality, was undertaken to make themselves more comfortable *in* prison—not to get *out* of prison. Few of them challenged their convictions in court and still fewer contemplated escape. They were too busy enjoying themselves.

This confounded the Old Heads, who could not conceive of a life beyond the walls so oppressive that it would cause all these strong and able-bodied young men to forfeit their freedom so willingly. Nor could the Old Heads win in their losing battle against the new prison subculture of young bucks who fought for prison turf as if it were their birthright.

To illustrate this conflict between generations, one of my closest Old Head friends was released from prison the day after he had slapped a young buck in the prison yard because "he didn't know how to talk to a man." Some time after his release, my friend was shot to death in a bar by that same young man, who had recklessly sought revenge beyond the prison walls with no regard for the consequences. The assassin has since been caught and now sits on death row.

The Meat Wagon Crew

By 1984, years after I had lost my clerical job, I was working as an infirmary janitor. Stabbings, murders, and serious injuries had become so frequent that the medical staff had had to form a special unit, to which I was assigned. Our job was to respond to the medical emergencies on the general population blocks.

They called us the "Meat Wagon Crew." When summoned, we would rush to the scene of a medical emergency, a staff nurse in the lead, one inmate pushing a gurney, another carrying an emergency medical kit, and a third bearing oxygen or medical equipment. While our crew was originally intended to serve as an ambulance service, it in fact more closely resembled a coroner's wagon. Two or three times a week, we could be seen rushing through the many long concrete corridors in response to an emergency call. Often we arrived only in time to remove a dead body or the unconscious victim of an assault.

In one case, an inmate had died of a drug overdose. He had frozen in a sitting position on his bed, his lifeless eyes stxm, aring out of a window. Inattentive guards simply added him to their usual count, while passing inmates wondered what could be so interesting outside. Finally, someone asked the stiff body that question, only to discover that dead men don't talk. When the Meat Wagon arrived, we had to struggle to get the rigid corpse out of the cell's narrow opening to the waiting gurney.

In most cases, if the medical emergency didn't involve a drug overdose, it was usually some aftermath of violence. One inmate, who had been attacked over nonpayment of a two-cigarette-pack debt, was found with his intestines spilling out from a razor slash across his stomach. We had to keep pushing his entrails back into place as we raced the gurney down the corridor. Another man's face had been so badly beaten that I didn't recognize him as one of my friends until a guard identified him from his I.D. card.

By 1985, the body count was so high that we stopped running to answer our calls. Regrettably, the helpless victimization of our fellow inmates and our own frustration had too long conspired to render us indifferent to violence.

Violence or degradation, self-defense or lost self-esteem, kill or be killed—these are not real choices. In the same way, Graterford offered no real choices to the multitude of men overcrowded within its walls. The violence of inmates was no worse than the brutality and insensitivity of an indifferent, omnipotent bureaucracy. In the long run Graterford's great walls would never be high enough to contain the hatred, violence, and rage swelling out of proportion inside.

Chapter 4

The Underground Economy

Editor's Note

The underground economy that the author describes in this chapter is a complex adaptive system. At the highest level, the system balances the supply and demand of goods and services. At the lowest level, it rewards and punishes the behavior of individuals. At intermediate levels, it responds in arcane ways to minor changes in the environment, especially changes in the "official" economy. When shortages appear in the official economy, the underground economy steps up production to fill the void. It assures inmates an uninterrupted supply of necessary goods and services, though at a cost. Although all inmates benefit from this underground economy to some extent, benefits are not distributed equally.

The underground economy also creates expectations among its component members, forming the basis of an underground society—a "Kingdom of Inmates" in this case—that is reflected in the spontaneous cooperative actions described in this chapter. Readers may wonder why, if the prison administration does not benefit from this underground economy, it allows it to exist. There is no simple answer to this question.

Drug dealers in prison often used homosexuals to smuggle and hold their contraband. For this reason, some homosexuals in prison enlarged their anal cavity so they could hide away greater quantities of contraband. Since many prison "mules" worked on a percentage basis, a larger cavity translated into more money. Some mules were even paid to carry the contraband in their cavities all day long. They became walking safe-deposit boxes.

By the mid-1980s, Graterford was in the advanced stages of a complete system breakdown. Not only had the prison become an extremely violent place, but the administration was showing signs of an inability to meet the inmate population's basic need for food and shelter. This breakdown, however, opened the door for a thriving underground economy which provided virtually every kind of goods and services that the legitimate prison system now lacked.

For example, if I wanted my laundry done, I could pay an inmate laundry worker with cigarettes to have my laundry picked up, cleaned, and delivered back to me. If, on the other hand, I had tried to send my laundry through the institution's authorized laundry system, I probably would never have gotten it back. Thieves and hustlers who profited from the underground laundry made sure that the prison laundry was unable to meet the population's needs. So for two or three 50-cent packs a week, an inmate could get his laundry cleaned and returned, which was a real bargain. Those who had no cigarettes wore dirty clothes or washed their own laundry.

Other black-market services abounded at Graterford, especially in the main corridor where most business was conducted. For a few packs a week, a swag man could deliver specialized cooked foods and pastries to your cell on a daily basis. The food was smuggled out of the kitchen by inmate workers who would then openly hawk them on any housing block. These swag men were the most prolific of the underground service providers and, since the food cost them nothing, also the best paid. The quality of bootlegged sandwiches was comparable to or better than that of the food served in the dining hall. But this said more about the breakdown of Graterford's food service than about the gastronomic skills of the swag men.

Eventually, I worked my way into a situation where my own basic needs were being met. I had at my disposal the eager services of swag men, laundry men, ice men (for summer ice cubes), barbers (to cut my hair in my cell), and phone men (to make sure I got signed up for phone calls). I could even have a cell cleaner, though I felt there were certain things a man should do for himself.

All in all, Graterford had become a predatory institution where nothing worked right and everything was for sale.

A Kingdom of Tribal Gangs

Through this gradual process of deterioration, Graterford the prison became Graterford the ghetto: a place where men forgot about courts of law or the differences between right and wrong, because they were too busy thinking about living, dying, or worse.

Reform, rehabilitation, and redemption do not exist in a ghetto. There is only survival of the fittest. Crime, punishment, and accountability are of little significance when men are living in a lawless society where their actions are restrained only by the presence of concrete and steel walls. Where a prison in any real or abstract sense might promote the greater good, once it becomes a ghetto it can do nothing but promise violent upheaval.

As weapons in Graterford proliferated, violence escalated, and gang leadership emerged, the administration gradually ceded control of the institution to independent gang tribes. During this period of gang expansion, there was no method to the madness. Violence was as unpredictable as the weather. By 1986, it was still epidemic, but it had more direction. Most of the violence was now directed at people who failed to pay their debts. The underground economy was so healthy at this point that it needed to take further steps in order to defend and preserve its fiscal survival.

Double D and Rocky

It is hard to find friends in prison, because most inmates are anti-social by disposition or through conditioning. One of the cruelest aspects of a penitentiary is the way it leaves one isolated and lonely despite the overcrowded surroundings. Yet, because of all the fear and hardship we experienced together, the friends I made at Graterford turned out to be my closest. The harsher the conditions, the closer the bonds between us.

Dan, my chess companion and one of my earliest friends at Graterford, was a quiet, soft-spoken man who stood a tall six feet and weighed about 180 pounds. His prison handle was Double D, an abbreviation for Dangerous Dan.

I had met Double D when I was in the county jail awaiting trial. For some reason he took a liking to me. I would prefer to think it was because of my dynamic personality, charm, and wit, but in prison such qualities don't account for much. Chances are, he liked me because he felt I was of some use to him. I've never really been certain why but, whatever the reason, I valued his friendship highly in those early years.

Dan never talked much, didn't lie, didn't steal, and didn't mince words. Though he belonged to no prison gang, he was respected by everyone. Those who didn't respect him feared him to the very marrow of their bones.

We both loved chess and, while he was a much better opponent, I played well enough for him to enjoy beating me. We played a lot on the block, because I didn't like being too far away from my cell. The good thing about chess is that it's not a spectator sport and is so boring to watch that it kept people away. Dan and I were able to have long, leisurely games and conversations without distraction.

"Why do they call you 'Dangerous?'" I once asked.

"Because they know I won't take any shit from any of these fleas."

"A lot of guys are afraid of you."

Dan rubbed his forehead and pushed up the brim of his everpresent prison work cap. Its tightly creased brim stood at a crisp 45 degrees to the ceiling, moving around like the dorsal fin of a shark. After a long silence, he replied, "I like it like that."

I must confess that being a friend of Double D's had certain advantages. One was the freedom to play chess without ever having to worry about an ambush or an attack, fairly common events in those days.

Once while we were playing, a mountain of a brute walked by. Dan never looked up, but I could sense he was watching the man's every move. I could also sense there was no love lost between them.

Rocky was the biggest and toughest convict in Graterford, and inmates and staff alike paid deference to him. He led a gang of black and white thugs called the "Terminators," which he liked to refer to as a paramilitary organization of anti-government terrorists. I had been told that Rocky's Terminators were the largest gang of extortionists, drug dealers, and smugglers in the prison. But to Double D, "Rocky's just another flea."

"You don't like him?" I asked one day after I made a rather stupid chess move.

"No. Pay attention to the board," Dan said in that soft voice.

"Why do you think they let him do the shit he does?"

Dan gritted his teeth with annoyance and rubbed his forehead, the shark fin of his cap circling the air. "Because he works for the prison. He's doing exactly what they want him to."

I had played enough chess with Double D to know his words were as complicated as his chess strategy.

"What do you mean?"

The fin came toward me. "This place only lets happen what it wants to happen. Rocky's no bigger than the 300 guards they got working here. That silly Terminator stuff is just bullshit. They use Rocky to keep everybody in line. He does their dirty work." Then he proceeded to beat me mercilessly on the chessboard, as if to emphasize his point.

According to Double D, Graterford had gone through some violent changes in the 1970s. Despite its rigidity and strict military discipline, three staff members had been murdered. One was a captain of the guard who in 1979 had had his head split open by a baseball bat in the main corridor. By the early 1980s, prison gangs had become firmly entrenched and the administration did not have the manpower or the know-how to deal with them. Furthermore, the rigidity and discipline did nothing to make their jobs any easier.

So, as Dan saw it, the administration decided to play a gambit: they relaxed the rules and, instead of trying to end the gangs, they manipulated them by playing one against the other. In this way gangs would be too busy fighting each other to work together against the system. To destabilize these gangs, the administration threw its support behind one gang to maintain a balance of power. So Rocky's Terminators became the administration's flavor of the month.

To me, this seemed too far-fetched to be the product of any rational administrative policy. Besides, it sounded illegal; you can't support corruption if you're paid to combat it. But in those days I knew very little about the prison system. So I discounted Double D's story, reasoning that the Terminators' success was more likely due to administrative ineptitude. The staff was simply as frightened of Rocky as were most of the inmates.

"Rocky's going to get himself killed," volunteered Double D one day, as he murdered me on the chess board.

"Why do you say that?" I asked, knocking my king over.

"Because people are getting tired of his bullshit. The administration can't protect him forever."

The conversation ended there. I couldn't imagine a thug like Rocky needing protection from anyone.

About a year later, gang wars broke out and numerous inmates were getting stabbed. Double D and I still played chess together regularly, but we were a lot more wary.

One day a friend of Dan's, Shorty, got beat up by Rocky over a phone call. Rocky wanted to use a phone Shorty was on, so he just picked up the little guy and threw him to the ground like a rag. Shorty was no coward, but Rocky was twice his size. It was a no-win situation.

Later that same day, Double D took the time to warn me: "Don't come out in the main corridor when they open up tonight. Just stay on the block."

But I was too young and curious, unable to imagine that the main corridor could be any more dangerous than it already was. When the evening bell rang, I locked my cell and ventured out, staying close to the guard's station just to play it safe. All seemed normal, except the traffic was extremely light. Too light for a prison of over 2,000 men. The main corridor exhibited a dreary glow, like the light of a fading fluorescent lamp.

Suddenly, the corridor became completely empty. A deadly silence gripped the scene. Some feet away, a guard ordered me back to my block as he scanned the corridor in puzzlement. Usually there would be last-minute stragglers loitering about, but now there was not a soul in sight.

As I started for B-Block, I felt a slight breeze. I looked up the corridor to see the auditorium door angled open—inmates were spilling out into the corridor. I was too far away to make out details, but I could tell that a huge mob was quietly filling the back end of the corridor and heading in my direction. It was an eerie, unsettling sight to see hundreds of men rush down a long corridor in utter silence.

Rocky happened to be coming out of the door directly to my right. When he saw the approaching mob, he ran as fast as a man his size could toward A-Block. He banged on the gate, yelling, "Key up! Key up!"

When the mob saw this, they all bolted in unison down the corridor toward him, shouting angrily.

The guard on A-Block, instead of retreating to the safety of the guards' station, courageously rushed to Rocky's aid, keyed the convict into his block, and locked the door behind him. Then in some fit of insanity he stood in the center of the corridor, raised his hand, and hollered, "Everybody back to your blocks! That's an order!" But the unstoppable mob ran over him on their way to confront Rocky and his Terminators.

Some men banged on the door to A-Block and screamed, "Key! Key!" Amazingly enough, another guard opened it and let through a stream of men before he realized his folly and slammed the door shut. The rest of the crowd streamed through the door from which Rocky had emerged moments earlier.

Leading the pack were Double D and Shorty. When he saw me watching in amazement from the corridor, Dan waved me away. His mob then disappeared into the dark doorway until all of them had emptied out of the main corridor. All that was left were me and the trampled guard still lying on the floor. Quickly guards hurried out of their station to drag their co-worker to safety. I myself rushed to the B-Block door and was lucky enough to be let in.

Soon the mob returned to occupy the corridor, hollering in triumph. This wasn't the Battle of Lexington or the Boston Tea Party, but the consequences were just as profound for Graterford.

No one was killed in this bloodless coup, but things changed rapidly. Rocky, the Terminator's leader, was transferred out of the prison that night. The next day, a number of his gang members were stabbed in separate incidents. Many of the others took self-lockup.

From that day forward, no one gang dominated at Graterford. If Double D's story was true, then the administration had lost its balance of power. Soon whole gangs of cell thieves were being stabbed and beaten. Just as these gangs had once made the administration superfluous, the collective will of the inmate population had now made the gangs superfluous.

Hence, the "Kingdom of Inmates" was born. Its new offensive curtailed much of the stealing which the administration had been unable to control. A collective conscience had risen among the inmates, as Graterford evolved from a ragtag nation of independent tribal gangs into a unified conglomerate of collective and competing interests. It was only a matter of time before the new kingdom would begin to test its boundaries by challenging the power of the prison administration.

The Inmate Code of Conduct

In retrospect, it was primarily the inability of Graterford's guards to ensure inmates' safety that brought about the demise of their control over their own prison. When things got so bad that inmates couldn't even commit themselves to protective custody, the population knew it had to fend for itself. The only thing guards could do for inmates now was to keep them locked in their cells.

Because of this, the population developed its own unwritten "Inmate Code of Conduct," which stood apart from the prison administration's rules and regulations. The Code went something like this: "Don't gamble, don't mess with drugs, don't mess with homosexuals, don't steal, don't borrow or lend, and you might survive."

By itself, this simple rule would never have worked unless something tangible and powerful prevented the inmates from killing each other and forced them to abide by it. That something was the flourishing underground economy. The black market of goods and services had grown so much as a result of overcrowding and failed security that a stable class of merchants and consumers had established itself within the prison population.

The swag man who sold me and others his sandwiches became my friend. But if it hadn't been so easy and profitable to steal from the kitchen, he probably would have ended up stealing from me. The more he provided his clandestine services, the more he created a demand, which in turn ensured him a steady income that was far less risky than breaking into another man's cell.

Every inmate in general population was either a buyer or a seller. It was now to everyone's benefit to abide by the Inmate Code of Conduct, so that the economic heart of the Inmate Kingdom could continue to beat.

The only threat to this economic stability, then, became the guards. Since they were no longer the mainstays of stability nor could they provide protection, their petty rules, shake-downs, and confiscations served only as an irritating nuisance that hindered the inmate population's new economic order. The Kingdom of Inmates had no choice but to challenge the authority of the guards in order to discourage their interference with the socio-economic balance.

Chicken Sunday

It is difficult to determine exactly when Graterford's guards yielded their authority to their charges, but one significant turning point took place on Super Bowl Sunday of 1983. An inmate left the C-Block dining room and headed for his cell, openly carrying a paper plate piled high with the usual Sunday chicken dinner and all its trimmings. It was his intention not to let his favorite meal interfere with his watching the Super Bowl on the TV in his cell. Posted everywhere around him were signs dictating, "NO FOOD IS TO LEAVE THE DINING ROOM."

While violations of this rule were commonplace, the usual practice was to hide one's food before leaving the dining hall. To accommodate this minimal demand for obedience, most inmates smuggled out food in anything from trash-bag liners to empty potato-chip bags, often stashed in the split lining of one's institutional prison coat. Guards never searched for food, and no harm was done.

But on this particular day, this inmate had decided to blatantly ignore convention. As was expected, a guard saw him with the food plate, followed him to his cell, and ordered him either to eat his food in the dining hall or throw it out. Considering the circumstances, this was a reasonable request.

The inmate told the guard in no uncertain terms that he planned to eat his Super Bowl meal in the comfort of his cell and there was nothing he could do about it. The guard, frustrated by this display of disrespect, grabbed the plate of food out of the man's hands.

What ensued became known as the Super Bowl Sunday Chicken Riot. Since C-Block housed many winemakers and this was a big sports day, a good number of the block's 400 occupants were drunk on hootch. When they saw this inmate's fight with the guard, everybody decided it was time to show the staff who was boss. Every inmate related to the incident as if the guard had tried to take away something of *his*. The chicken was more than just food—it represented each man's hustle, and its confiscation challenged everyone's livelihood.

Dozens of men swarmed to the aid of the inmate and beat the guard. Dozens more mobbed the dining room to defiantly take chicken dinners back to their cells. In quick order, every guard on the block was assaulted and some were even locked in cells.

Notably, the inmates attacked only guards and not each other. Not a single inmate was hurt in the uprising, which made this event uniquely different from other prison riots. If anything, the inmates actually joined together with a coherent plan. Some seized a guard's radio transmitter and called for reinforcements, while others armed with sticks and clubs waited in ambush by the block's main entrance. When a dozen or so guards rushed into the block, inmates fell upon them like swashbuckling pirates and quickly subdued them. Then they locked their new victims into cells.

What happened next was the most convincing proof that a kingdom had arisen. The inmates abused and humiliated the guards— but they didn't seriously injure any of them. Once they were satisfied, they simply opened the main door to C-block and allowed other guards to tend to their fallen comrades, just so they could see what might one day await them. Some inmates even assisted the nursing staff in tending to the wounds of guards they had attacked only moments before. There were no demands for better conditions, amnesty, media, the superintendent, or anything else.

And that was the end of the Super Bowl Sunday Chicken Riot. Most of the inmates simply returned to their cells to watch the Super Bowl Game, drink jailhouse wine, and eat chicken. Nothing else happened for the rest of the day. At the 5:00 p.m. count, everyone locked up in their cells as usual. It wasn't until then that guards quietly gathered the rebellious inmates from their cells and escorted them to the Hole.

By then it was too late. The point had been made. Inmates had joined together to defeat the guards fair and square. The interests of the inmate population had been advanced and defended, thus ensuring the livelihood of each and every man in the triumphant Kingdom of Inmates.

To this day, Graterford is still the most violent prison in the state system. It now houses over 4,000 men and is home to the most politically active inmate population in Pennsylvania. If you ask any staff member or inmate who runs Graterford, the answer will always be the same: "The inmates run Graterford."

Chapter 5

Prison Politics

Editor's Note

In this chapter, Hassine describes how a prison's political system operates on a day-to-day basis. Unlike the underground economy, which thrives on change, the political system opposes change of any sort. While the staff is generally not allowed to participate in the underground economy, some (though not all) of them are willing participants in the prison's political system.

From the author's perspective, inmates and staff who have this political participation in common tend to benefit from the status quo. By resisting change, the political system maintains the status quo and ensures that those few who are on top today stay on top tomorrow. The main differences between participating inmates and guards are the methods each uses to maintain this status quo. As described by the author, a prison's political system does not seem much different from the political systems encountered in other contexts.

> "What we got here is a failure to communicate!"
>
> —Strother Martin
> *Cool Hand Luke*
> Warner Bros., 1967

The process of change within the prison system can be as treacherous as the most notorious of its inhabitants. The danger associated with navigating the murky waters of jailhouse politics makes that change sometimes very difficult to control.

Change in society is inevitable, but in prison there are powerful competing groups of differing interests with much time on their hands and a strong motivation to prevent particular changes. A prison's very existence often depends on the struggles to control change. Its soul is not reflected by the preciseness of its construction nor the orderly appearance of its uniformed staff. Nor does the calculated chaos and deliberately random violence of its inmates necessarily expose the real belly of the beast. Only on the battlefield of resistance to change will one be likely to find the naked prison as it exists in today's reality.

Much like soldiers in combat, inmates and prison staff have little overview of the arena where their conflicts play out. They can only glean narrow glimpses of it from the small plots of turf they happen to occupy at any given moment. Consequently, inmates and guards alike can never afford themselves a complete view of the prison in which they live, work, and struggle.

In any prison system, the parties of competing interests are represented by the inmate population, the rank-and-file uniformed staff, and the managerial administration. The interaction between these three groups defines a prison at any given time. Those few times when all three parties are in agreement over some particular change, the result is a quick and effective integration of that change. Likewise, when all three parties are completely united in their opposition to an impending change, the result is unanimous rejection, even though other unrelated and unexpected changes might occur because of competitive tactics employed by one or more of them to resist the original change.

By far the most common and most volatile type of change in a modern prison comes as the result of two groups attempting to impose change over the objections and resistance of the third group. Even though the decision of the majority will be upheld, the resisting minority will nevertheless be relentless in its attempt to undermine that change. The end result is most often some dysfunctional change where conditions are worsened by the minority's resistance. Thus, the intended change is never fully realized. Reluctant change is always more destructive, because jailhouse politics tends to maintain and perpetuate any ongoing struggle.

The Sergeant, the Major, and Me

One illustration of the complexity of prison politics was revealed to me soon after my ill-fated hamburger caper in 1981. There was an unexpected consequence to that infraction of which I was not initially aware.

After my misconduct hearing, I returned to my cell to begin serving my 60 days of cell restriction. At the time, I genuinely felt I was being mistreated. Compared to the rampant thievery and abundance of violence I had witnessed in Graterford, my measly infraction was hardly worth the bother. Losing my job and paying for the burgers made sense, but two months locked in my cell for 22 hours a day seemed unfair to me.

Little did I realize that there were higher forces who felt I had been treated too leniently and who wanted to thrust me into the lions' den of jailhouse politics. In actual fact, stealing food from a penitentiary kitchen was a serious offense because it involved two vital concerns of the administration: spending and control. Graterford spent an average of $2.75 per day to feed a single inmate, in contrast to the statewide average of about $2.10 per day. To the powers that be, the ease with which I was able to buy smuggled food from the kitchen meant that the prison could not control its inmates. If other inmates similarly challenged its control, the per diem cost of feeding the population could rise drastically.

Ten pounds of bootlegged ground beef should have landed me directly in the Hole. The fact that I used the Major of the Guards' bathroom in my plot normally should also have cost me double time in cold storage for my arrogant defiance of authority. If anything, cell restriction was a lucky break for me. But what did I know? I hadn't been in prison long enough to appreciate the seriousness of the situation.

When I finally arrived at my cell, I was unexpectedly greeted by the B-Block Sergeant. A man of military bearing, he stood a rigid six-feet tall in a starched and precisely creased uniform. His prison dress cap added height to his authority.

"Didn't think I'd be seeing you back so soon," the Sergeant said, chewing on a lump of tobacco in his cheek that gave his southern drawl a lazier tone. He spat to accentuate his words.

I assumed he was referring to my returning so soon from the misconduct hearing. Usually men given cell restriction took their time coming back in an effort to extend their liberties.

"I got 60 days cell restriction, Sarge," I complained naively. "Can you believe that?"

The Sergeant spat again. "Boy, the way I see it, you must be a real important inmate to have talked your way out of the Hole. I don't like important inmates on my block, so you just watch yourself because you can be right sure I'll be watching you."

With that, he double-locked me in and walked away like a general who had just reviewed his troops. Amazed by his hostility, I foolishly thought he was singling me out for some personal reason, perhaps because I was Jewish.

However, the truth was that the Sergeant's attitude had nothing to do with me but with my former work supervisor, the Major of the Guard, who had intervened on my behalf to keep me out of the Hole. This recently appointed officer happened to be the only African American in Pennsylvania history to hold such a position. As such, he was the first member of a minority to personally direct the actions of an historically all-white guard force at Graterford. Additionally, he had been promoted from the rank of Lieutenant, which was not only unprecedented but caused a stir among the several Captains he was promoted over.

To further complicate the situation, the Major was also a reformer, a compassionate and decent man who did not feel that physical force was the way to solve Graterford's problems. In his view, such a traditional style of prison management often led to the unfair treatment that had thrust Graterford into a crisis in the first place.

While the prison administration and the overwhelmingly African-American inmate population were hopeful about the Major, the almost all-white, rank-and-file staff were disgruntled over his appointment. Not only had a longstanding race barrier been broken, but there was genuine concern that the Major's management style would give the prison away to the inmates. Militarism and white leadership had been the way at Graterford for generations.

When the Major had decided that my actions were not serious enough to warrant sending me to the Hole, battle lines were drawn. Derogatory slurs were already being made about him by the uniformed staff, often in the presence of inmates, which only served to undermine the Major's authority.

There I was in the middle of all this, and I didn't even know it. I simply wasn't yet tuned in to the political undercurrents sweeping through Graterford.

While on cell restriction, I was let out of my cell for two hours each day for recreation. During this time, I found myself and my cell constantly being searched by the block guards. Though they were not as intrusive as they could have been, even one search of a man's cell or body is an assault on his sense of dignity and freedom.

Naturally, my resentment and paranoia grew with each search, as if every guard was out to get me. Helpless to stop them, I began to hate these men in uniform. To make matters worse, some of them would ridicule and taunt me by calling me the "Major's boy." At times they would even imply that I had avoided the Hole by being a snitch. The mere suggestion of such a label in a prison like Graterford could have been potentially life-threatening for me.

On the 59th day of my 60 days of cell restriction, I was issued another misconduct—for taking more than two hours for recreation. Reporting to another misconduct hearing, I was given an additional 30 days of cell restriction. As I returned to my cell, the Sergeant was again waiting for me.

He spat a wad. "Boy, I don't know why you came back to this block. You got no job and you just keep breaking the rules." He spat again. "You must know some real important people. But let me tell you this. Let any of my officers catch you wrong again and nobody's going to be able to save you then."

This time I said nothing, though I'm certain the hatred beating in my heart could be heard by the Sergeant as he locked me in and paraded out of sight. For all my frustration and anger, I was too young and inexperienced to realize that his malice was focused elsewhere. The old soldier was just trying to stop the process of change. His real enemy was the black Major with his liberal notions. I was just someone who was unlucky enough to be chosen as the vehicle for his resentment.

Resistance to change in a prison can foment enough resentment and malice to result in changes so riddled with compromise and disregard that more problems are created than solved. The only beneficiaries of this kind of change are those who will profit from the system's breakdown. As a 15-year veteran of jailhouse politics, I can now only speculate what could have transpired had the Sergeant approved of the Major. Could Graterford have become a better place? Could I have become a better person? Unfortunately, what could have been is now just a silent, unfulfilled prayer.

The Politics of Anger

I always considered myself a proud American and, despite my incarceration, I still subscribe to the traditional American system of values. Before coming to prison, I expected it to be a very unpleasant place, staffed by the otherwise unemployable and inhabited by the generally unredeemable. While I was not surprised by the amount of violence and corruption at Graterford, I was genuinely shocked by the level of persecution.

The Sergeant did much to shape my current reality. He accomplished this by continuing to have the block guards pat me down and search my cell, even after I had completed all my cell-restriction time. Generally, this type of treatment was reserved for troublemakers and drug dealers. I was neither. Though the searches never turned up anything of consequence, my cell was always left in total disarray. My creature comforts, such as an extra pillow, bed sheet, and towel, were taken away from me.

Beyond the unfair treatment, the Sergeant had succeeded in making me feel even more isolated from the world that existed outside the prison walls. I was no longer so proud to be an American. I was just a convict without rights. But again, I had simply misconstrued the motives behind his actions.

When prison guards feel they are losing control, their first response is to crack down hardest on the segment of the population over whom they still have control. This is done as a show of force to let the general population know that they mean business. Furthermore, if cooperative inmates are being treated this harshly, then the troublesome ones can expect much more serious treatment.

The problem with this control tactic is that it doesn't always work. Often the uncooperative elements of the population don't necessarily get the message or don't care about the consequences of their actions. When this happens, conditions usually worsen. There is still a control problem, only now it exists with the added hostility and resentment of the more stable inmates.

I was now made to feel the full weight of forced confinement in an imposed egalitarian police state. All my life I had been taught to work for my livelihood; the harder I worked and the more resourceful I was, the greater would be my reward. But now everything was turned around. No matter how hard I worked, or even if I worked at all, I received the same portion as everyone else. There was no incentive to achieve anything or improve myself. In fact, the more well-behaved I was, the more likely it was that I would be mistreated by inmates and staff.

Prison anger affects every aspect of prison life and management. At Graterford it made victims of the Major, the Sergeant, and me. We were all left wondering what kind of world we had fashioned and, each in our own way, resented having to live in it. While anger usually demands satisfaction, it often settles just for company. I had now resolved that the inmate population would be my new nation. And the first thing I would do was join the Graterford Lifers Organization.

Omar and the Lifers Group

"I need a pass for the Lifers meeting," I told the guard seated at a small, shabby desk in the middle of the B-Block "Bridge." The Bridge was a ten-foot walkway that spanned the two upper-tier walkways of the block like the center crossline of a big "H." Behind me stood 20 other men waiting for their passes off the block. I spent a good deal of my time at Graterford waiting in one line or another.

"I didn't know you were a lifer," replied the weary, disaffected bridge officer, a phone receiver cradled between his shoulder and ear. Routine had just about made him a part of the furniture he was stuck in. His hands quickly fingered my inmate I.D. card, but he never looked up. He knew me only from the identity photo.

Without answering, I silently waited for my pass. He slid back to me a standardized slip of paper and my I.D. card. I took both immediately and headed down to the ground floor of B-Block.

Once I reached the block's main entrance, I waited my turn in yet another line, this time for the front-door officer to allow me off the block.

"I didn't know you were a lifer," the door guard said, echoing the bridge officer.

Again I waited silently until he decided to verify my pass. I then entered the main corridor and merged with a moving mass of inmates. During general movement, hundreds of men walked quickly up and down the corridor. Most of them wore prison uniforms for work or exercise clothes for the yard, but there were always some in pajamas and bathrobes whose only apparent purpose was to be part of the confusion.

As I headed for the auditorium, I could hear the familiar voices of hustlers hawking sandwiches, drugs, and anything else worth selling. Hundreds of voices bounced off the concrete walls, the usual disconcerting din which always heightened my concern that I might accidentally collide with the wrong guy. Sometimes the carnival atmosphere here made me forget the dangers of this place. But invariably, I would witness the all too common corridor knifing and be reminded once again how risky it was to commute on this prison's main boulevard.

Halfway to E-Block, I arrived at the main entrance of the auditorium, one of its four doors wedged open with a guard blocking the way inside. I gave him my pass, which he glanced at and quickly returned without a word. All his attention was focused on the many shadows speeding past him in both directions. There were no other guards in sight, so his safety was more of a priority than me. Besides, who would attend a Lifers meeting if he wasn't a lifer?

Crumpling the pass and tossing it, I stepped inside into a dusky twilight. The auditorium, used on weekends as a movie theater, had its lights dimmed down to ambush dark. This would explain why the door guard chose to take his chances in the more brightly lit corridor.

A few feet inside, I was greeted by the first row of steel-framed theater chairs. The auditorium could seat about 1,000 men in three descending columns of these battered folding seats. Deep within was a flat area of space flanked by two basketball hoops mounted on the wall. Directly adjacent to this was an elevated stage that stood a few feet off the floor. It had a large, dirty white projection screen pulled down in front of it.

As I looked down at the farthest row of seats, I could see about a hundred indistinguishable figures either standing, sitting, or slouching. Three men stood alone together, facing the audience.

I couldn't make out anybody I knew well enough to sit next to, so I just walked down to the third row and took an aisle seat. Soon after, I heard the sound of a heavy steel door slam and lock. Shut in from the noisy corridor, I was unaccustomed to such eerie quiet.

"I call this meeting to order," said the tallest of the three standing men.

I had never been to a Lifers meeting and I wasn't sure I wanted to be there now to listen to some of Pennsylvania's most vicious killers. But since I'd become one of the boys, I decided it was time to meet my fellow lifers. Besides, I longed to be a part of a self-governing body.

There were three inmate social organizations in Graterford at the time: the Lifers' Organization, the Knights of Henry Christof, and the Jaycees [Junior Chamber of Commerce]. Each of them were allowed to raise funds in the prison through the sale of food or by providing services, such as showing movies and taking photos in the visiting room. Prison gangs would inevitably dominate these groups and try to control or manipulate any money-making ventures that they undertook.

As the tall man spoke, everyone appeared attentive. The meeting followed a reasonable order of business, with questions asked and politely answered. I soon felt so completely at ease that I wanted to join the discussion in some way.

The tall man gave the floor to the shortest man, apparently the financial officer, who started giving a business report. I knew the lifers sold soda and potato chips to the population on weekends during the auditorium movies. What I didn't know was that they were allowed to make profits and maintain a bank account. I was thrilled to hear that a private enterprise zone actually existed in Graterford. Maybe a little too thrilled.

When the speaker concluded his report, I enthusiastically stood up and asked a question. "Excuse me, I heard you say we have money in a bank account. I just wondered, how much do we have on deposit and how much revenue do we generate?"

I don't know why I stood up but, from the sudden focus of attention on me and the mumbling around me, I realized that standing up in a Lifers meeting meant a lot more than I had intended. Things got ugly real quick.

"Why do you want to know?" asked the speaker.

"Well, I just wondered how much money we were making," I replied a little defensively.

"What are you, a troublemaker?"

"What are you talking about? I asked a simple question and I'd like an answer." Instinct had trained me not to let anyone talk down to me.

It was obvious I had hit a nerve. The prudent thing would have been to sit down quietly and forget the whole matter. But prudence in Graterford was seldom a viable option since it was often mistaken for weakness.

"Why don't you sit down and dig yourself," said the tall speaker.

At this point I felt a tugging at my shirt sleeve. An older man in his mid-forties materialized in the seat beside mine, smiling up at me. As my focus was on the escalating trouble in front of me, I just pulled my arm away and answered the speaker.

"I'll sit down when I get an answer."

The tall man took a step toward me, and I turned toward the aisle to confront him. Once again I felt that tugging at my sleeve and glanced over at the widening smile of my neighbor.

The short speaker reclaimed my attention. "Look, why don't you just sit down."

Someone behind me called out, "Sit the fuck down, motherfucker!"

Then someone else shouted, "Answer the man's question!"

Things were obviously getting out of control, as my fellow lifers now tried to egg on a confrontation. Painfully, I knew I would have to remain standing until I got an answer, no matter what happened.

The third man, who had said nothing so far, finally broke his silence. "Look, all of this noise is going to get the guards into our business." Then he addressed me, "Now look, I ain't never seen you at a meeting before. I don't even know if yc 're really a lifer. Besides, we ain't got this month's statement yet."

The three then began to speak among themselves. The tallest one had to be pulled back from advancing toward me.

Before I got a chance to decide what to do, I was pulled down into my seat by the smiling man. He never gave me a chance to speak.

"You are either the bravest man I have ever met or the dumbest. It's too early to tell which." This wasn't said offensively, and the man's demeanor was so kindly that I had to appreciate his sense of humor. But I still kept one eye on the three speakers.

"Now just sit where you're at and try not to say anything," he continued. "You made your point. What you need to do now is take a look behind you and see what you got started. Those three guys up there are really not your major problem."

Cautiously I glanced back. I was surprised to see how many men were standing up and looking in our direction. There was a lot of cursing, mumbling, and even a few snarls. I turned back around.

"What are they all so mad about?"

"Mad?" The smiling man belly-chuckled. "They're not mad. They're just warming up."

Almost on cue, one of the men directly behind us stood up and hollered, "You know *I'm* a lifer, motherfucker, now you tell me about that money. And don't give me no shit about you don't know. You ain't pulling that on me. This ain't my first time here."

Someone else shouted out, "Man, don't be feeding into that negative shit. Sit the fuck down!"

Yet another voice called out, "Man, fuck that! What's wrong with knowing how much money we got?"

The guy directly behind me answered, "They stealing, that's what's wrong."

"So who ain't?" shouted a faraway voice.

A dozen men were now arguing among themselves, some holding others back. It looked like a fight was about to break out at any minute. Nevertheless, my companion just continued to smile as he shook his head.

"It sure doesn't take much to get these men started," he said.

Still a little confused about what was going on, I just looked at him in silent amazement.

"Let me ask you a question," he said. "Did you happen to notice that the guard locked us all in here with no supervision? Do you know why he did that?"

I shook my head.

"Because he knows that everybody in this room has at least one confirmed homicide to his credit. And obviously being smarter than us both, he decided he didn't want to be caught in a dark room alone with a bunch of murderers who might start fighting. Now tell me, what do you suggest we do if things turn ugly?"

His words left me speechless.

"I thought so. You haven't got a plan. You're just playing out of pocket. Well then, you might as well tell me your name so, if I get my old behind in a tussle, I'll know who to thank."

It took me a moment to answer. "My name's Victor, but I really didn't mean . . ."

"It's too late to sweat it now. I just hope you can fight as good as you can talk, because you managed to embarrass some of the men in here."

"But all I did was ask a question."

"That's all it takes in this place. People don't like to answer a whole lot of questions, especially about money, especially if they're stealing. I'd be surprised if they weren't. By the way, my name is Harold, but I prefer to be called Omar. I don't like being called by my slave name." With that he extended his hand to me.

I gladly shook Omar's hand. It looked like I might be needing a friend. Besides, there was something about him that I really liked and admired. Nothing seemed to rattle him.

To both our relief, things were settling down. Almost everybody was sitting down now, though with a cautious edge.

"Why does everyone seem so angry all the time?" I asked my new friend.

"Good question. It's probably because most of the men in here take everything personally. Nothing's really personal unless you want it to be. Or it could be that anger is really all the authorities leave you that's your own. They take everything else away from you at Receiving. Now, why don't we start easing toward the door so that, when the guard decides to open up, we can slip out of here without getting our feelings hurt."

With that sage advice, Omar and I got up and walked up the aisle. He was smiling and chuckling, which took some of the tension out of the air, occasionally calling out or waving to one of his friends.

Once we made it to the auditorium door, Omar turned to me and said, "Victor, you live a charmed life. You may even manage to come out of this with a little rep [reputation]. In the future, try not to upset anybody and always make sure you have a way out before you start asking questions. Frankly, you like things a little too exciting for me."

In time, Omar and I became as close as brothers. The population would come to know us collectively as the Muslim and the Jew. And it was through Omar's wisdom that I learned that nothing in prison is personal.

Chapter 6

Race Relations in Prison

Editor's Note

Race is a constant in many prisons. An inmate's race may determine where he can stand, sit, or work, or what he can say and to whom. In many prisons, race-based rules of behavior are common, and minor infractions of the rules can have serious consequences. Knowing these rules is part of becoming a convict. As one might suspect, race-based rules lie in the purview of the prison's political system and are part of the status quo. But as Hassine points out, race can be transcended by other factors.

Race relations between prisoners and guards are a more complicated issue. Other things being equal, the racial make-up of a prison's staff is determined by the racial make-up of the locale. Thus, prisons located in rural areas tend to have predominately white staffs, while urban prisons tend to have racially mixed or even predominately black staffs. This generalization usually excludes the effects of affirmative action programs, unions, and organizational philosophies, which can further complicate any sociological analysis of prisoner–guard race relations.

"... A gang leader in Philadelphia has led Graterford's Muslim movement, officials said, controlling part of the prison's drug trade. A prison guard, Lieutenant Cynthia Link, said that when the lights in the prison's mosque suddenly went out one night two years ago, the 100 inmates ignored her order to leave. Finally, one of them

> said, 'Ms. Link, these people aren't going to move until
> [the gang leader] tells them to.' Link said, 'Well, go
> gethim, tell him I need him.' He came, told the prisoners
> to leave, and they did. . . ."
>
> *The New York Times*, October 30, 1995
> [Complete article reprinted in Appendix B]

Every Pennsylvania prison that I have been to, regardless of the ratio between black and white inmates, was operated by an almost entirely white staff. In Graterford between 1981 and 1982, over 80 percent of the staff were white, while over 80 percent of the inmates were black. By July 1987, according to two Pennsylvania Department of Corrections surveys on a racial breakdown of inmates and a corrections-workforce comparison, the disparity remained relatively the same with 76 percent white staff and 76 percent black inmates. To its credit, however, Graterford employed the highest percentage of minority employees out of all of Pennsylvania's state prisons.

Though the prison had been desegregated since the late 1960s, the inmates of Graterford continued to impose their own form of segregation. For example, it was an unspoken rule that the dining hall be divided into a black section and a white section. The administration did its part as well, for example by refusing to double-cell white inmates with black inmates. De facto segregation was very much alive in those days, as it is today.

At Graterford I observed that many of the new white guards had little experience interacting with people of different races. Presumably due to feelings of intimidation or discomfort with inmates of other races, they tended to be much stricter with those of their own race.

During my initial classification period at Graterford, I was required to identify myself as either white or black. There were no other options. Hispanics and Native Americans were classified as white or black at their own choosing. It wasn't until the mid-1980s that the racial classification process at Graterford allowed inmates to designate themselves as anything other than black or white.

Among the African-American population at Graterford was a large and well-established Black Muslim community, the vast majority of which came from Philadelphia. On the other hand, most of the white prison staff were Christians, many of whom were raised in the rural communities around the prison. This extreme imbalance between the racial, regional, and religious composition of staff and inmates vividly reflected the general dysfunction of the prison that prevailed throughout my years there.

Though non-white inmates were usually embraced by the prison population, they were often considered suspect by the white staff who seemed to reserve the benefit of the rehabilitative doubt only for white inmates. This racial bias at Graterford did not result in favoritism by staff but rather provoked a divisive and relentless competition between the inmates themselves for the staff's favor. Everyone in the prison system was forced to play the bias game, because the only group identity available to inmates was based on skin color.

As a rule, a prison administration is reluctant to promote any group activity or identity that might evolve into a clique of gangs. Graterford was solely in the business of confinement, so its entire security force was geared toward discouraging and punishing any group affiliations. All inmates were issued identical uniforms, and there were strictly enforced rules against any congregation of more than five inmates. While some social and religious organizations were permitted to operate, the administration made the rules of participation so cumbersome that these groups constituted an organization in name only. Though the prison could not punish an inmate for belonging to a legitimate group, it could try to weaken his desire to belong. One of the ways in which this was accomplished was to influence every inmate, including myself, in the direction of racial polarization.

Black and White Prison Gangs

Generally, black gangs in Graterford were extensions of Philadelphia's neighborhood street gangs. They bore names based on their urban location; for example, the 21st and Norris Gang, the 60th and Market Gang, the 10th Street Gang, etc. Many of their members had belonged to the original street gang before they were incarcerated. Once sent to Graterford, they joined their prison counterpart to carry on the gang's traditions. As more and more street-gang members arrived, their growing strength in numbers enabled them to conduct a wider array of prison-gang activities.

The moment any African-American Philadelphian entered the prison, scouts immediately approached him to determine which part of the city he came from and whether he had been a member of a street gang. This sorting of incoming blacks based on geography dictated the character of black prison gangs, giving rise to the often used term "homey" for those who hailed from the same neighborhood or hometown. Homeys were the most common recruits for black-gang membership.

Black gangs competed vigorously with each other for turf and the control of contraband sales. While this competition often resulted in violent battles, gangs on many occasions merged their enterprises and worked together. For example, rival gangs had been known to fight each other over the business of selling drugs, yet they frequently cooperated in bringing the drugs into the prison.

Those black gangs formed by inmates from areas other than Philadelphia differed considerably from the black Philly gangs in that, for the most part, they had no counterparts on the streets. Such non-Philly gangs usually originated in the prison and their members were often strangers who happened to be from the same county or city. The competition between regional gangs and Philly gangs tended to be very hostile and violent. There was seldom any trust or cooperation between them. Numerically, Philly gangs greatly outnumbered other gangs, which allowed them to dominate the population and completely exclude outsiders from joint ventures.

Regardless of their numerical superiority, it is highly probable that Philly gangs still would have had more control, because their carry-over from street gangs gave them the distinct advantage of functioning under well-established rules, organizational structures, leadership systems, and ideologies. In contrast, regional or prison-based gangs tended to be weakened internally by frequent power struggles, uncertain leadership, and untested organizational processes.

Because Graterford's black gangs were determined almost exclusively by geography, gang membership was widely diverse. In any one gang you could expect to find drug addicts, thieves, murderers, and hustlers of every ethnic influence, including Muslims,

Christians, and atheists. This amalgam of homeys provided black-gang members with a sense of commonality so dynamic that the administration was very hard pressed to break them apart.

Black gangs at Graterford primarily operated as money-making enterprises. While geography helped to bring prison gang members together, it was money and drugs that kept them together. The goal of every gang was to earn money, which meant selling anything that anyone was willing to buy. As in a corporation, gang profits were then reinvested to buy more contraband for further distribution. Gang members gauged their individual value by the amount of money they were able to make. What they did with their earnings was of no consequence, since the hustle itself seemed to be all that mattered. Money earned was merely an indicator of how good a hustler an inmate could be.

White gangs at Graterford were a completely different story. These gangs almost always originated in prison and, like the non-Philly gangs, were not as well-structured or established. They too were comprised of members who were often strangers to each other, most of them brought together by the simple chance of their skin color.

Statistically, white gangs in Graterford were strictly a minority, usually formed for their own protection from other gangs. While they might be involved in some hustling, they were limited by their inability to protect their turf or business interests against the larger black gangs. They were more likely to be the buyers of drugs and contraband than the sellers.

Furthermore, most white gang members were not brought together by geography but rather out of a need to protect their mutual interests. White drug addicts tended to join together in order to pool their funds to buy drugs at a volume discount. Some white gangs were formed because of ethnic bonds, such as Catholics, Italians, and Protestants, or because of special interests, such as gamblers and body builders.

White gangs at Graterford were more likely to be small, improvised groups rather than organized teams with specific agendas, and were generally much less diverse than their black counterparts. Whereas black gangs required large memberships to generate income and protect their turf, white gangs preferred to have as few members as possible in an effort to stretch their resources. Any white

gang that grew too large would promptly be challenged by the domi-
nant black gangs.

The exceptions in Graterford were the outlaw motorcycle gangs
that successfully managed to entrench themselves within the prison
system. Like the Hell's Angels who had already established themselves on the street, they were far more business-oriented and could
compete directly with black gangs in the sale of contraband, drugs
in particular. Despite their relatively small numbers in the prison,
their connections to the much larger street gangs made them resourceful money-makers and a power to be reckoned with.

The Muslim and the Jew

Not long after my first Lifers meeting, Omar became my closest
friend and my window into the workings of prison life. He knew
many of the inmates at Graterford and understood better than I the
language, games, players, and dangers of the prison system. Most
importantly, he was willing to share his wisdom with me. His profound insight into the system helped me to grope my way through
a foreign country of which I had had no inkling before I arrived at
Graterford. Thus, Omar became my Old Head and I became his
eager disciple.

A few months after I had lost my job in the Major's office, Omar
was hired to take my place. Since he now lived on the same block
as I did, I often visited him in his cell. We ate meals together, walked
the yard together, and exchanged a lot of jailhouse philosophy to
kill time. We became inseparable and were one of the more unusual
sights in Graterford: the veteran black Muslim from Philadelphia
and the young Jewish rookie from New Jersey. We were constantly
arguing about one issue or another.

I would often find my Old Head sitting on the cold, hard concrete
floor of his cell, deeply absorbed in writing a letter to his family but
never turning his back to the doorway, always keeping one cautious
eye on the inmate traffic a few feet away. His cell was drab and
spartan, containing little more than state-issued clothing, bedding,
and some old newspapers. I once asked Omar why he chose to have
so few possessions.

"I don't like people taking things away from me," he replied. "If
I don't have anything in here that's mine, then the authorities can't

take away any more than they already have. Besides, I don't think it's healthy for a man to get too comfortable in the slammer."

On one occasion I had just returned from a prison basketball game that had ended in a vicious melee between a black and a white gang. Often one prison gang would field a team to play against a team backed by another gang, and the rivalry on the court usually led to violence. Watching who won the game was only half as exciting as watching who won the fight *after* the game.

But today I was particularly disturbed by the rampant hatred and racism between black and white inmates, so I posed a naive question to Omar: "Why do they hate and hurt each other so much? Why don't they just get together and channel their hatred toward the guards?"

Omar's ubiquitous grin vanished. After a long stare that was pregnant with pause, he finally said: "It's all a game."

"What, that's it?" I protested. "All the beatings, stabbings, and killings are just a game? It's no game. Men dying is no game."

Omar regarded me with some amazement. I must have been a bit more excited than I had intended. With a gentle but serious tone he cautioned, "Are you going to argue with me or are you going to listen?"

I sat quietly, waiting for him to share his view of the restless shadow we lived in. Just outside his cell, silent, unfriendly faces glided past, glancing inside, never smiling. It was this kind of backdrop that kept a man alert in his cell at all times. Occasionally a prison guard would look in on us and then move on. Though I was not allowed to enter another man's cell, the rule was never enforced.

"Most of the hate and anger in here is all a game," Omar emphasized again. "It's a hustle, just another way for people to make money. Anger and hatred are a prison's cash crop.

"When whites hate blacks, they're stealing the sympathy and favor of a mostly white Christian administration. When blacks hate whites, they're strong-arming appeasements and concessions. The administration, they get the most out of it all. Violence and hatred in prison means more money, more guards, more overtime, and more prisons. What incentive is there to keep prisons safe and humane? All staff has to do is sit back and let the men here tear each other apart. Then they can cry to the legislatures and tell them how much more money they need to control their prison. Just like with the prison swag men, dope boys, and laundry men, there's something being sold and money being made. Only it's a lot more money than most of the guys in here can ever imagine. It's a lot easier for everyone to profit from hatred than it is to help the poor and ignorant do something positive with their lives."

I couldn't believe what I was hearing. "Come on, Omar, you can't believe that stuff. You're sounding real paranoid, like there's a conspiracy everywhere." His views were similar to those of Double D, who believed the administration was actually encouraging gang activity. But I wasn't ready to believe either one of them. The prison system was too chaotic to be that deliberate.

Omar replied, "Well, then you tell me why, with all the guards, guns, locks, gates, walls, and money, they still can't stop what's going on in here?"

I had no answer to that. "Okay, if this is all a game and everybody knows it, then why do the men in here play it? Why do they play when it can get them hurt and even killed?"

Omar smiled assuredly. "It's like a Dodge City crap game in here, Victor. Everyone who plays it knows it's crooked, but they play it anyway—because it's the only game in town."

Chapter 7

Saying Goodbye

It was a hot summer day one particular weekend. Most of the inmates were wearing non-prison sweat suits, sweat shirts, or ragtag gym clothes homemade from scraps of stolen cloth. Many of them chose to spend all their recreation time on the block, most of them serious gamblers or avoiding the sun or those avoiding a fight.

The gamblers were the easiest to spot because they always played cards on the most private picnic tables in the deepest interior. To a man, they slumped low in their seats, ready at a moment's notice to reach for their weapons. These weapons were usually hidden somewhere below the table, waiting for someone to be caught cheating or prematurely grabbing another man's money. Most other block loungers just milled around, talking, smoking, or drinking coffee as if they were somewhere other than in a maximum security prison.

I had just returned to my cell to change into state whites for my infirmary job. To me, the only difference between hard labor and imposed idleness is the change in a man's appearance. In the end, both will break a man's spirit as surely as his sentence will make him older.

As I left my cell, I heard a distant commotion from the upper range. Hearing it too, the table gamblers slumped a little deeper in their seats, easing closer to their weapons, their eyes never leaving their cards.

Soon I could make out an inmate called Hammerhead Fred, running toward me down the narrow walkway of the tier above, with guards in hot pursuit. He was carrying a five-gallon plastic bag, the kind used to dispense milk from a cafeteria cooler with a rubber nipple on one end. But this one was filled with homemade jailhouse hootch.

As he ran the length of a football field, Hammerhead lifted the bag over his head and forced the booze to flow into his open mouth. Much of it poured onto his face and chest, glazing his protruding forehead and staining his dirty clothes. The heavy bootlegged load was slowing him down, and the pursuing guards were gaining on him.

The whole cellblock was in an uproar, every man cheering him on. "Go Hammerhead! Fuck those hacks! Drink that wine! Don't give it up! Hammerhead! Hammerhead! Hammerhead!"

Just as the lead guard caught up to Hammerhead, an inmate suddenly stepped out of his cell and "accidentally" collided with the guard. The two fell down, and the other guards toppled over them in Keystone Kops fashion.

This gave Hammerhead enough time to take an extra long swallow of hootch. Then he jumped off the second-story walkway and landed upright on a tabletop below. Amazingly, he managed to hold onto his five-gallon bag. His legs spread boldly across the table, Hammerhead guzzled more wine until he had had his fill. Then he hurled the container at the frenzied crowd around him, beat his chest, and gave a savage victory cry.

The crowd screamed, hollered, and beat their chests as they drank from the contraband container, passing it from man to man in a victory-sharing ritual. Finally, the guards got themselves together enough to force Hammerhead down from the table. The inmates booed and hissed as they escorted Hammerhead away, no doubt to a waiting cell in the Hole.

But Hammerhead couldn't have cared less, because he was too drunk to feel any pain and more importantly because today was his last day in captivity. He had served all ten years of his sentence, and he owed no parole time or probation. He was out tomorrow, free and clear.

This was how Hammerhead wanted to be remembered and how he would always be remembered. This is also how I have always remembered Graterford and its Kingdom of Inmates, since the day I myself said goodbye and good riddance to its wretched concrete walls.

PART II

Interviews

Editor's Note

In this second section, Victor Hassine presents a series of interviews with fellow inmates, each with a specific theme. These
personal views serve to broaden the author's perspective on
prison life. Readers should be aware that in some cases the interviews have been heavily edited to disguise and protect the true
identities of the interviewees, but the interviews themselves are
largely verbatim.

Chapter 8

Interview With David: A Sexual Victim

Editor's Note

The following interview with David is a troubling piece. The interview was intended not to pass judgment but to accurately portray a man's transformation from youthful innocence to a life of victimization. The catalyst here is what Hassine has called "senseless violence," of which David is a sad product.

I first met David, my current next-door cell neighbor, in Grater-ford. He was starting a two-to-five-year sentence, and I was two years into my life sentence. David was 19 then and "cute as a bug in a rug"—a curse for any young man in prison.

At the time, I was working as a clerk in the Chapel, which was how I met David. It was there that he was assaulted and raped repeatedly by at least three men. I was present to see the aftermath of young David's introduction into Graterford's criminal justice system, one of many lessons on the facts of life in prison society.

It is now about ten years later. This is David's second time back in prison, my fourth transfer to a different institution. We both have landed in SCI-Rockview, which is a medium/minimum security prison in the mountainous central region of Pennsylvania. Rockview is considered to be one of the less restrictive "soft stops" in the Pennsylvania state prison system.

It was here not too long ago that another attractive young man like David was gang-raped by four of his weight-lifting buddies.

The head "booty bandit" [jailhouse rapist] was named Pac Man, also a cute-looking youth when he first rolled into Graterford to do his time. Ironically, the same "beef rustlers" who raped David in the Chapel had also "long-dicked" Pac Man a year or two earlier. This is but one of many examples of prison's vicious cycle of victims-turned-attackers.

David was gang-raped not once but twice. Now in his late twenties, he has served close to half his life in institutions and has made most of the important decisions of his life based on the experience interacting with inmates.

David's story, a grim portrait of today's incarcerated youth, presents a too-common slice of prison life that is sadder than many of the broken men who are my neighbors, and sadder still than the prison pallor that greets me in the mirror every morning. The following is excerpted from a 1991 interview.

"[In the county jail I had] sexual pressure, fighting over my manhood. I was playing chess for money and lost several times, and it became like a 20- or 30-dollar debt. I couldn't immediately cover it. I was given a choice, either borrow it or have sex with him. We got into a fight. [After that] he left me alone. . . .

"There were a couple of guys who tried to take me under their wings, but I didn't really trust them. I had heard stories about this. The ones who wanted to take me under their wing I didn't even know until I went to jail. It was strictly a con; [these guys] were like predators. . . .

"When I got to Graterford, I took protective custody lock-up 24 hours a day. A guard came down one day who had a pass for me to go get legal mail. He unlocked my door and left. I got up out of bed in my underwear and was rushed by approximately six or more inmates. I was raped numerous times. They rushed me, then threw me to the floor and hit me a few times. Before I had a chance to react, a knife was placed at my neck. I was already on my side or stomach. I don't remember what was said. I somewhat knew what they wanted and it wasn't my commissary. All they did was fuck me with no emotion. I was hoping while this was happening that they would ask me to have oral sex and I would then bite them. Had it been under other circumstances, I would have fought back. At that time I was in good shape. I would guess logically that it was a set up.

They left as soon as it was over. I was angry, bleeding, and in quite a bit of pain. Because I was in protective custody and it happened there, the point in telling or reporting it was pointless and also very dangerous. . . .

"I lost all hope for about six months. I was totally stripped of emotion. I just didn't give a fuck anymore. When I was much younger, I was a vengeful person. But I didn't want to get even because where there is an action, there is always a reaction. . . .

"I don't think it was fair that I was raped, because I did nothing to deserve the vicious assault that has haunted my mind for almost ten years. They had no right to victimize me, for now I have become a product of that assault. It has caused me to become attracted to other young men sexually, so as to continue the nightmare by further subjecting myself to punishment for my past crimes, and to also inflict my nightmare on others so they too can carry the terrible burden I've carried. . . .

"The administration could have done more to protect me, or others that are in protective custody, by totally segregating them, which ultimately wouldn't be fair, because you would be deprived of all activities enjoyed by the regular inmates. But, on the other hand, isn't this the same reason most of us are here, for depriving those of society of their normal routines and enjoyments of life? Basically these types of occurrences can be avoided by tighter security for these young individuals, because most of the booty bandits are already known by the administration. Again, these occurrences are so commonplace that the administration often looks the other way, unless the person who is victimized is willing to put his life on the line and prosecute the perpetrators. The reason I say the perpetrators, instead of the guilty ones or rapers, is because most of these individuals are products or victims themselves. . . .

"After the first time I was raped while in protective custody, I convinced the officials to let me out in population without telling them that I was assaulted. They let me out into population and I ran into a friend who I met on the street. I hung around with him for a while, figuring he could teach me the ropes of survival in the "Big House." He introduced me to a fellow who was too nice, who one day invited me to the Chapel to get high. I met him, and he had a few friends with him. We smoked a couple of joints, and the next thing I knew I was getting physically beaten and again was viciously raped by at least three guys. . . .

"After I was raped, the only medical attention that I received was a physical examination of my rectum to confirm that I had been assaulted. I was placed back in protective custody by myself without anyone to talk to, alone and deserted like a dirty rag. I received no therapy from either a psychologist or a psychiatrist. I was left to deal with it on my own. I didn't cry out then because no one seemed to care, and so I stripped myself of all and any emotions. If there were people who cared, they really didn't come forward, which is natural, because it is a very difficult thing to respond to. I can sympathize with women victims. It is a devastating experience to not only cope with, but even more to live with. . . . I am only recently able to start to deal with it because I no longer suppress it, as it is causing me to now go through a sexual identity crisis. . . .

"Once I was released from prison, I was very demanding of people because I felt they owed me something. And more than often, if my wishes were not complied with, I took what I desired from them. Don't get me wrong, I never raped anyone, but I did lash out on all the supposed predators and even those, both family and friends, who I felt deserved to be tormented. I didn't discriminate. I did it to anyone I felt had it coming to them. Anyway, that was how sick I was then, or rather that was how obsessed I was, until recently. Now, mostly I feel guilty about what I've done in an act of retaliation. But I also realize I was really crying for help in the only way I could, by acting out.

"I am a very confused person now, sexually that is, because I am insecure about what is natural combined with what I've been through and seen with my own eyes through the many years that I've been in institutions, 13 years altogether. I am attracted to younger guys because of their innocent look and naive personalities, more so because it's that very innocence that I was robbed of. Sometimes I feel really guilty after I have sex with a guy, because I know or feel that I have violated their minds subconsciously, and eventually they'll have to face the music about who they are or cop out and remain a victim. But I am realizing that all that is happening is that I am doing it because that's the only way I can get any kind of love, affection, and/or attention that I so desperately need.

"[As for the system], I still don't trust them because they are the true predators and rapers of the people."

David is getting out soon. I wonder whether he will find that desperately needed love, affection, and attention in the outside world. And if he doesn't, I wonder what he will do.

Chapter 9

Interview With Chaser: A Medication Addict

Editor's Note

Prescription medications are ubiquitous in many prisons, and chlor-promazine tranquilizers are common in virtually all these institutions. Other medications, such as amphetamines, barbiturates, and diazopene tranquilizers, are routinely dispensed. Although these medications are given to inmates under the supervision of a physician, the actual distribution is often handled by guards and fellow prisoners. Since these prescription medications are readily available, their role in the underground economy is small. Any prisoner with a prescription can hoard pills, of course, and sell or give them to others.

The author's opinion of prescription medications and their use in American prisons is apparent in his interview with Chaser. Whether one agrees with him or not, medications have become part of the status quo in most prisons. Given the increasing use of penal institutions for housing the mentally ill, it is unlikely that the prevalence of prescription medications will abate in the near future.

I met Chaser in 1984, my fourth year at Graterford, when he first arrived to serve time on a robbery conviction. I can still remember the frightened look on his face that first day. As I was adapting to the rapidly changing rules and conditions of a prison in total meltdown, Chaser became the beneficiary of my hard-learned lessons on inmate survival. We managed to forge a mutual friendship.

Many outsiders who have met Chaser would comment, "He doesn't look like he belongs in here." I've heard this often when people encounter an inmate who doesn't have some grotesque feature that neatly fits their preconceived notion of the "criminal look." Experience has taught me that the less an inmate appears like a criminal, the more likely he is to be particularly vicious and unrepentant. Criminals who look like criminals keep people on guard; the honest-looking ones put them at ease, which allows them the greater advantage of misjudgment. But in Chaser's case they were right. He didn't belong in prison, let alone deserve to become a victim of the system.

I did my best to look after my friend until, about nine months later, he was transferred to the Rockview facility. This was a relief for me, since protecting a naive and scared young man from the predators at Graterford was no easy task.

Once he was transferred, I quickly forgot about Chaser. Frankly, it is nearly impossible for me to remember all the people that have come in and out of my life, especially nowadays with the influx of so many frightened young kids. Almost all my relations with fellow inmates today are superficial, as prison life becomes more and more a case of every man for himself.

What Chaser and I didn't know at the time was that prison administrators were feverishly trying to figure out how to stop the imminent collapse of Graterford and other overcrowded prisons. With thousands of new, young Chasers coming in, it was becoming more impossible to feed, house, and clothe them all, let alone rehabilitate them. More importantly to officials, an increasing number of guards and staff were becoming victims of inmate attacks. As employee safety was their first priority, the administrators realized that something had to be done to shore up the cracks in Graterford's foundation—and it had to be quick, cheap, and effective. But Chaser and I never concerned ourselves with the administration's problems. After all, we had swag men to deal with and predators to avoid.

In 1990, as I made my way to chow at Rockview, I ran into Chaser again. He was walking out of the dining hall's special section reserved for the "nuts" whom the administration referred to euphemistically as "special-needs inmates." Chaser walked sluggishly with a disheveled, glassy-eyed appearance. In short, he *looked* like one of the nuts.

"Chaser, is that you?" I asked.

"Hey, Vic," he replied, "I've got to talk to you. It's real important. Meet me in the yard."

That evening in the yard, my old friend explained to me how he had returned to the streets two years earlier, only to lose his wife and son, develop a voracious drug habit, and end up committing burglaries to support his habit.

I was unmoved by Chaser's story, since almost every returning con I've ever met recounts a similar tale of woe. All I wanted to know was why he was on the nut block and why he was taking "brake fluid" [prescribed psychotropic medication]. It was obvious because of his very slow, disjointed movement and his shakes. Another alarming clue was the noticeable scars on his wrists from razor cuts.

Chaser described how his return to prison had exposed him to the "medicate-and-forget-them" system of modern prison maintenance. This new system of mind-altering and mood-altering psychotropic drugs was rapidly becoming the prison administration's "quick, cheap, and effective" solution to warehousing masses of inmates into smaller spaces, while using fewer and fewer support services.

The reasoning seemed to be that every dose of medication taken by an inmate equaled one less fraction of a guard needed to watch that inmate, and one less inmate who may pose a threat to anyone other than himself. Hence, overcrowding had brought about a merging of the psychiatric and corrections communities. The resulting effect on inmates can be best described by Chaser during this 1994 interview.

"The first time [I came to prison] I was terrified because I didn't know what to expect and I knew no one. I was awkward and didn't know my way around. I had not acquired a prison or inmate mentality. The second time I was much more at ease because I knew a lot of people still in prison and I knew what to expect. I had also learned quite fast how to become as comfortable as possible. I had to take a lot of psychotropic drugs to achieve this comfortable state of mind. . . .

"In November of 1989, after telling the shrink in the county prison that I wished I was dead, I was unknowingly given Sinequan which knocked me out for three days. But since I was in a special quiet section of the jail, I continued the medication, because to me it was better than being in population. . . .

"I think the biggest difference between street drugs and psychotropic drugs is that street drugs give me some kind of feeling of well-being, high, confidence, euphoria, and contentment. But psychotropic drugs cause all feeling to cease. It stops self-awareness and sucks the soul out of a man. It slows or stops a man from striving to better himself and he stops caring about everything. It also creates total laziness. That laziness becomes his entire attitude and also is 100-percent habit-forming. . . .

"After almost three months at the county prison in Philly, I was sent to Graterford to start my four-to-ten-year sentence. I had abruptly stopped taking the Sinequan and felt totally disoriented. I lasted three weeks in population. Looking for drugs, I ended up taking another inmate's Thorazine at times. I was out of control and all I could think of or look forward to was getting stoned.

"One day I got very drunk and went into a blackout and refused to lock up. Four guards carried me to a room and I was put into restraints. I was given nine months in the Hole. I did five at Graterford and was sent to Rockview to complete it. . . .

"[Getting medication in Rockview] was quite easy. I said I wished I was dead, which was the same thing I said in the county. Every week the shrink would ask, 'How do you feel now?' All I had to do was say, 'Bad,' and ask for more or different meds. I always got what I asked for, as long as I told them I thought of killing myself. . . . I took Sinequan, Melloril, Elavil, Klonopin, first separately, while always asking for Valium. Then in desperation, I mixed the medications and the dosages. The ultimate effect was total numbness. My body was numb. My feelings were numb, and then my mind was numb. I did not care what happened to me and just stopped thinking about anything. . . .

"While taking the meds, I was put on a special block and given a single cell. I got only a reprimand at misconduct hearings and did not have to go to work. I felt I was being placated and given special attention and I liked that. But when I stopped taking the meds, I was shook down [cell-searched] a lot and went to the Hole if I was ever given a misconduct. Once in the Hole, I would say I wish I was dead, and again they'd give me medication. . . .

"I admitted to staff many times that I had a severe drug addiction and that I had an abusive personality. I tried numerous times to get in the drug-therapy groups and on the D and A [Drug and Alcohol] Blocks. I was refused and ignored every time. . . .

"I lost all sense of dignity and self-worth. I had no pride. I lost all interest in the outside world and eventually did not care if I ever returned to it. All I knew or cared about was what times I went to get my fix and hurried to be first in line. I constantly had the shakes and inner tremors. My speech was slurred and slowed, and so was my thinking. I could not think ahead. I was like a small child only looking for instant gratification. My entire metabolism changed, and I gained a lot of weight fast. It damaged my memory, even to this day. . . .

"Since I was under constant supervision and being evaluated once or twice a month, pre-release and parole became much harder to obtain. So for the luxury of being comfortable and in a fantasy world, I had to abandon the idea of early release or furloughs. Since my number-one priority was no longer a goal, it became easy for me to forget or stop striving for what was once important to me. The side effects of the medication, such as tremors and shakes, made it impossible for me to get and keep a job. Education, reading, learning, and working to strengthen my mind became things of the past. Giving up became repetitious and habit-forming (not unlike street drugs) and eventually I lost and gave up my self-respect, dignity, and morals until my only interest in life was getting in line three times a day to receive my medication.

"I had given up on all these things, and I woke up one day and realized I was a very sad man. But I was willing to give up on life, because the medications I was taking made me think I was comfortable. . . . I had given up on Chaser. . . .

"I was seeing a shrink two times a week because I was depressed. I was not diagnosed as having any kind of mental illness or chemical imbalance, but despite that I was taking large dosages of Thorazine, Sinequan, Lithium, Elavil, and Melloril. I took them at 7 a.m., 11 a.m., 4 p.m., 8 p.m. . . .

"One night just before lockup, I got another misconduct. I didn't care if I went to the Hole or got cell restriction. What concerned me was that the administration might possibly take away my medication. So after weighing my options, it seemed only logical to kill myself, or at the least, give that appearance. I opened my window, pressed my wrists against the frozen bars, then took an old razor and opened my wrists. I figured that, if I died, that would be fine. But, if I lived, I would definitely get more medication, and that thought satisfied me. I lived this madness and insanity for well over a year, until I ran into you. You offered me your time and energy to explain to me what I was doing to myself and what I was becoming. Within six months, I was totally off the special-needs block and off 99 percent of the medication and my will to live and succeed returned . . . with a vengeance. I never needed the medications for my depressed condition. I just needed someone to say they cared. I needed a friend. I got both from you. I owe you my life, not the prison, and not the medication. . . .

"I have been medication-free for two years now and, although I'm usually uncomfortable with prison conditions, I can look in the mirror and see Chaser looking back with a smile. So to me, giving up the medication was a small price to pay to be myself again.

"[Psychotropic medication] is one of the easiest things to get in prison. It is easier to go to the shrink and ask for 500 mg of Thorazine than it is to get on the phone or get a pass to the Chapel. If a guy goes to the doc saying he feels depressed, violent, or suicidal, the doc will give him one of numerous medications. He is usually given a choice. All the medications are geared to slow a man down or fog his thinking so bad he can't think of why he's depressed, violent, or suicidal. This will continue for years, as long as he says he needs the medications to a staff person once a month. . . .

"I'd say 40 percent of the population here is taking some form of psychotropic medication. They are treated less harshly than those unmedicated. They are seen and talked to by staff much more often than those not on medications. They are given special consideration at misconduct hearings. They are permitted to come in from night yard earlier than the other inmates and, in a lot of cases, are given a single cell. When it comes to working, someone on psychotropic medication can usually pick whatever job he says he can handle. On the other hand, most of us were not required to work at all. . . .

"I believe that, when a guard or any staff member puts on a uniform, they know it stands for authority. So they demand respect and control. When someone rebels or stands up to them, they feel their authority and control is threatened and they take steps to eliminate the rebellion. They put on the appearance of power, so they act cold, mean, negative, and harsh to display this power.

"Now when a guy is on medication, the threat is almost nonexistent. They [the staff] feel safe and secure with the men that are medicated. So the use of force and display of power is not necessary, and they act more leniently to the medicated inmate. They treat these men like children. To staff, a medicated inmate is a controlled inmate and not a threat to them. . . .

"[If all inmates were required to take psychotropic drugs], I would be shocked and scared. It would be like they were turning the prison into a brainwashing institution. I would think they had lost all control and were attempting to gain it back by stopping our wills and brains from functioning properly. I believe they are headed in that direction because of how easy the medications are to get and how many people are taking them. . . .

"I think that, as the prison populations continue to grow and grow, and a younger and more violent crowd comes in, it will become harder and harder for the administration to control all the blocks. I think they are now learning that the best way to control inmates or pacify them is to totally medicate them. It may even become a reward system."

Psychotropic drugs are nothing new to the psychiatric community, which has been using them on the mentally ill for years. However, its use in corrections as a population-management tool and behavior modifier is relatively new. The effects of prolonged use of such medication on an ever growing number of inmates are unknown.

Just from the increasing size of medication lines and the growing number of inmates doing the brake-fluid shuffle, I have observed that psychotropic medications (also known as "chemical shackles") are defining the behavior of an increasing percentage of inmates in the general population.

As politicians and bureaucrats continue to debate the loftier issues facing the criminal justice system, the mother of invention has required front-line prison administrators to quickly implement any practice that might help them to keep their prisons intact and functioning. The practice of medicating inmates is rising fast up the ranks of prison-administration hierarchies, since it has proven to be a relatively inexpensive and efficient prison-control tool. The two governing estates of custody and treatment are being pushed aside by the rising third estate of psychiatric medication.

A bureaucratic system that subdues whole populations with drugs must certainly give us pause. The wisdom of turning means into ultimate ends in this way needs to be questioned. Today in prison, I find myself longing for any glimpse of an attempt to rehabilitate, not because I believe in rehabilitation but because I worry about a society that no longer bothers to consider its possibility.

In my opinion, today's prison managers are only interested in their ability to contain an ever-increasing number of people for an ever-longer period of time. Since there is only so much that can be done in terms of cell and prison design, the search for solutions has focused not on changing the nature of prisons but on changing the nature of prisoners. With medication, breaking down a man's mind is much easier and more economical than breaking ground on a new institution. Besides, if a prison system only has to develop a more cost-efficient way to create a better inmate rather than a better citizen, who would really know the difference? Who would really care?

As of this interview, Chaser has been off medication for about two years. He has successfully gone through drug-rehabilitation therapy and is soon due for release. Once released, he will join a growing number of mind-altered men who are leaving prison and entering the mainstream of society. Only time will tell whether chemically treated inmates do in fact make acceptable citizens. But, if you ask me, we should go back to trying to build a better mouse trap and, for God's sake, leave the mice alone.

Chapter 10

Interview With Toney: An AIDS Tragedy

Editor's Note

Although the proportion of gay inmates is unknown, it is most likely greater than the proportion of gay men in free society. This disparity is observed despite a pattern of benign discrimination against gays in many prisons. For example, openly gay prisoners are often denied access to programming and employment opportunities "for their own protection." This pattern has expanded steadily since the onset of the AIDS epidemic. In this context, the following interview with Toney provides rare insights into the mind of an openly gay inmate. Readers with personal experience with AIDS prevention may recognize the air of despair in Toney's words, while others may by shocked by his explicit frankness.

Toney is a young, homosexual inmate dying of AIDS in a Pennsylvania prison. In his own words, he takes us through the gauntlet of prison life which has beaten down his spirit with all its ordeals of love and hate, crime and punishment, and compassion and indifference.

Unlike the multitude of other incurable diseases afflicting mankind, AIDS not only threatens our emotional and physical well-being but tears at the very fabric of our society. It is for this reason that AIDS can devastate the uninfected living as mercilessly as it already has its living dead. Equally ominous is how AIDS has served as a catalyst to the social changes brought about by the ills of promiscuity, drug addiction, crime, violence, and incarceration.

In this 1992 interview, Toney relates how the lack of education about AIDS affects homosexual activity in prison, and how it is used among the inmate population as a tool for self-destructive love or as a weapon of hatred that can be deadlier than a concealed knife.

"My being gay in prison [has put] a lot of pressure on me from men constantly wanting to have sex with me because of the way I look, which is on the attractive side. They constantly beg me for either a blow job or anal sex and are most of the time willing to pay for it. A gay person can be treated like royalty in prison. Homosexuals have the choice of making it easy or tough. . . .

"It is very easy to have sex in prison, at least for me it was and is. The only difference that varies from prison to prison is where you may have to do it and how careful you have to be about being caught; for example, at Graterford you could lay up all day with another man and have sex without being bothered by the C.O.'s [correction officers]. Whereas, [at Rockview] you're lucky to get a good nonstop fifteen minutes of sex. Yet it still happens. Some days in prison I have 20 men a day. . . .

"I can surmise when I may have contracted [AIDS], but I cannot say for sure. I've been an active IV drug user for 21 years, a homosexual all my life, and had a blood transfusion in 1985 before there was the start of screening blood. So you see, I cannot pinpoint it and I've had thousands of sexual partners and most of them were for one-time shots or night only, and I used to prostitute. I do know when I first got sick in the fall of 1986. I had a tremendous loss of weight and night sweats. I had all the symptoms and that was while I was in the Philadelphia Detention Center. . . .

"I had the test taken in 1987. I was a little stunned, but I was expecting my blood test to come back positive. Why? Because of the impact of the symptoms I had in 1986 at the Detention Center. . . . The reason I say I was only stunned was that, at the time I was told, I didn't realize the seriousness of what I had. . . . A normal person's T-cell count is 2,000 or more. Mine is down to 88, and I am considered to have full-blown AIDS. . . .

"The prison administration didn't give me any support when I was first told. No physical or psychological help. I was only told to stop having sex and that, if I was caught having sex, they would put me in the Hole. They did nothing to help me in any way for the remainder of the 18 months I had left to do. I didn't get any help until I went home and went to a specialist who prescribed AZT and Bactium to try and prolong my life. That's when I realized the seriousness of my illness and that it was a matter of life or death. . . .

"I sincerely believe [the prison administration] should have more accurately informed me—by the proper medical staff—of what I had and what could happen or couldn't happen. There should have been more facts given to me than the words 'don't have sex.' With this type of illness, a person, or I should say myself, should have been more educated on what was necessary to try to maintain life for as long as I could and the prevention of getting sicker. And as a result of just being told not to have sex—without strict reasons— I continued to have sex and more than likely infected others who infected others. At the time I was not aware that AIDS could so easily be passed from one person to another. I believed that you could not get it from oral sex or that sex with the same partner only a few times was safe. I was wrong because of the lack of education, or should I say no education, from the prison administration. If they can tell you you're slowly dying, they should also give you the facts as to what can harm others as well as harm yourself. . . . I remained sexually active [for two years] until I was educated by doctors on the street and read and educated myself about AIDS. . . .

"I now realize the dangers that are involved in having unprotected sex. So, therefore, I have made it a way of being a part of my everyday living of being honest and direct with anyone who asks me, whether it be a sexual partner or someone asking out of curiosity. I explain as well as inform others of the risk involved in dealing with someone like me, with the illness that I have. Even as I warn them, my partners usually don't care whether they get it or not. All they're concerned about is loving me or making love to me. I have allowed myself to be in relationships where no protection was used, and it is not because I did not tell them. It is because they wanted to be a part of me and make lifelong commitments to me. Or they wanted a lifelong commitment from me. So once they started having unprotected sex with me, it was my spouse's way of saying, 'You belong to me forever.'

"This happened with my last spouse whom I love very much, and we didn't use anything. So he now has [AIDS] and he knew all the risks. Yet he wanted it that way, so I allowed it to happen. He has a life sentence and he wanted to die and lay side by side with me in a coffin when I die. He did it out of love, and I thought I let it happen out of love. I realize that what we did was the insanity of being human beings. We were both wrong, or more so me, for allowing it to happen. But there's a saying, 'love can sometimes be blinding,' and in this case it was true. Because I loved him, and yet I hurt him. I learned not to let my emotions overcome my reality. . . .

"I know some associates of mine who are out to get revenge on people and are passing [AIDS] on. A homosexual I know says he is going to kill as many people as possible. I'll never understand it, but that is the way human nature is and the way some of us accept or cannot accept life's situations. It happened and there is very little chance of a person knowing whom to hurt anyway. So they want everyone to hurt as they hurt. I myself may have gotten AIDS because of someone not caring and out to kill everyone else. I'll never know. . . .

"I am doing this [interview] of my own free will, because I care for human life. Also so I may make people more aware of what a person that is HIV positive can feel, cope, and deal with it. Also to enlighten the minds of others with or without AIDS. And to let people know that prison is not a way of life and AIDS is not either and is no joke. . . .

"[If I were standing in front of the Governor of Pennsylvania], I would first tell him that it should be mandatory to ask inmates if they want to be tested for the HIV virus. Not mandatory testing, but mandatory to ask inmates if they want to be tested for the HIV virus. That way it can stop the spreading of a lot of illness and death in prison, because a lot of inmates have it and don't know it because they're not tested. Even though the administration doesn't condone homosexual acts, it is a fact of life that goes on, and I believe I would tell him to supply condoms to inmates. Just by issuing condoms doesn't say that everyone should go out and have sex, because there are a lot of people that don't mess around. But it would save lives in prison and in the streets. Sex is being practiced at an alarming rate throughout the prison system. And if it is going to happen anyway, why not make it safe?

"And I would also tell him inmates are transmitting the disease rapidly among themselves and then allowed back into society to spread it even more. Think of the men who have it and make HIV babies. The reason that is happening is because inmates don't know they have it because they were not tested. And also there should be medical specialists that deal in infectious diseases and not just a medical doctor who gets all his information from pamphlets and books and seminars. A doctor treating HIV patients should work and have firsthand knowledge of dealing with the disease. That's what I would tell the Governor."

This interview frightened me, not because it threatened my moral beliefs or my conservative way of life, but because it threatened my very *life*. AIDS has bound us all to Toney, because the virus which is eating away at his immune system is also eating away at our ability to trust each other. We are becoming as unforgiving as the deadly disease itself.

We can no longer welcome the stranger, pardon infidelities, or excuse even our own indiscretions. Our nightmare of the hopelessly desperate AIDS carrier has forced us to live in a purgatory of doubt and distrust, limiting our lives to the certainty of condoms, blood tests, and our own fidelities.

Toney died of AIDS in 1994.

Chapter 11

Interview With Albert Brown: A Permanent Resident

Editor's Note

The author's interview with Albert Brown skillfully contrasts the old with the new. In the old days, prisoners lined up in an orderly rank and file for every daily routine. A sort of silent system was routinely enforced with sanctions that verged on corporal punishment. By contrast, the new prison today is a place of remarkable laxity, disorder, and anarchy.

Today's prison, which is supposed to be the bastion of the status quo and the hallmark of uniformity, is changing faster than one can possibly imagine. There are more inmates and more prisons than ever before. There are women guards, doctors, lawyers, gym coaches, and teachers working in prisons today. There are even children in prisons. What would an Old Head who has spent a lifetime of incarceration think of these rapid changes?

Every day when I rushed out of my cell on some busy agenda, I always passed an elderly black neighbor quietly and contentedly sweeping the range floor. The only reason I even noticed him was the steady routine of his life was in stark contrast to the fast-paced upheaval around him. He seemed so impervious to it all.

Then one day I observed him explaining to a much younger man how he would be willing to relieve him of his burden of doing time.

I sensed there was more to this very Old Head than met the eye, so I decided to interview him.

Albert Brown is a 74-year-old lifer who looks more like he's in his late fifties. He stands a tall six-foot-one and has a deep, strong voice that hints at a hearing problem. One of the most impressive things about Mr. Brown is his air of honesty, something you don't see very much of in prison.

Listening to his observations about prison life past and present, I learned why Mr. Brown cares little about change and even less about the rest of the world. As I watched this man, it was hard to resist the feeling that I was looking at the face of my future. I shuddered at the possibility that he represented the natural consequences of a lifetime in prison.

When Mr. Brown first came to prison in 1945 at age 25, separate but equal was the law of the land in the relations between blacks and whites. It was a very different world when he started serving his life sentence in Philadelphia's Old Eastern Penitentiary, which was built in 1829. In 1958, he was transferred to Western Penitentiary, which, when it opened in 1826, was the first of its kind in the world. In 1962, he was transferred back to Old Eastern, where he got into a fight with a white man. To avoid trouble, he asked for a transfer to Graterford Penitentiary and arrived there in 1964.

Prison Then

"At nine o'clock a guy would blow a trumpet and all the lights would go off and it was time to sleep. At six o'clock they would blow that trumpet again and it was time to eat breakfast. You would have to hurry and line up to eat. You better not butt in line or go out of place like they do today. No sir, you couldn't do none of that back then. . . .

"Whites and blacks were segregated. We were completely apart. There were about eleven blocks and they were almost even blacks and whites. All the cells were double-celled then. . . . I never went to other blocks so I don't know what happened in the white blocks, so I have to say everybody was treated the same. The white guys always got the best jobs. . . . Everybody ate the same thing. Even the guards would eat what we ate. . . .

"No dayroom, no TV, no radio, or nothing. They gave you headphones that plugged into a plug in the wall. There was no newspapers and you were lucky if you got over an hour of yard when you got yard. There was no gym equipment. Nothing like that. The only magazine they would let you have was the Christian Science Monitor. People could write, but it was censored going and coming. . . .

"They had a library you could go to sometimes in the afternoon, but they only had some old books. Plus I couldn't read too well then. Blacks worked on the blocks as janitors or in the kitchen. All labor jobs. . . .

"They had novelty shops then. Inmates made things and they were allowed to sell them. Some had a big business with people coming and picking up their things regular. Some people would work for others. But only whites were allowed to do this. Sometimes if you had the right connection you could work for a white guy and make some money. . . .

"I could barely read or write. I went to school, and it was inmates who taught me how to read and write. Inmates did almost everything back then. There were inmate nurses, clerks, and teachers. There was even an ex-inmate pharmacist. He had been pardoned. Only whites had these jobs. We did have one black that did machine work. But the rest of us did labor. I worked in the laundry. . . .

"In 1956, there was a riot in Western Penitentiary. The inmates took control of the prison for a few days. After they took the prison back, the governor hired a new commissioner to clean up things in the prisons. He made a lot of changes for the better. They hired two black guards for the first time. One of them quit and soon returned to prison as an inmate. He said he quit because he couldn't lock people up. He's still at Graterford today, I think. . . . In 1960-61, the commissioner ordered an end to segregation. The Warden at Graterford refused to integrate. They fired him and forced desegregation. There was a few fights after they desegregated but no big problems. People didn't like it but they lived with it. . . . Afterwards, it was inmates that kept the dining room segregated. I remember there were people written up for not wanting to sit with blacks or whites in the dining hall. . . . I can't really say whether desegregation made things better or worse. They are pretty fair now. If there is racism, it is the inmates, not the prison. . . .

"I remember in the Sixties I watched them put double cells in Graterford for the first time. The commissioner was there and he looked at it and said it was too small for two people and made them move them all out. He changed a lot of things for the better. . . .

"I never knew how important *Gideon* [the landmark case of *Gideon v. Wainwright* that established an accused criminal's right to counsel] would be. Before then, people couldn't come near any law things. They'd get in real trouble if they even tried. . . ."

The Hole

"I was in the Hole at Old Eastern. I got two slices of bread at nine o'clock and two slices at three o'clock. No lights. A half a blanket on a metal bed. . . . The Hole weren't no joke back then. No, sir, they didn't fuck around with you back then like they do now. If a guard writes you up, they'd lock you up right away in your cell and just tell you what you done wrong. Nothing complicated and official like you get now.

"After a few days in your cell, guards would come and get you out of your cell and take you to the Deputy's [Deputy Superintendent of the institution] Office. You know, back in them days the Deputy ran the prison. He wasn't like a figurehead the way they are now. Anyway, if the Deputy wasn't available, the Major or Captain took his place.

"The guards would take you to a waiting room off the Deputy's Office. Then they'd make you stand facing the wall with your nose on that wall. And you'd better not take that nose off that wall if you knew what was good for you. Those guards had them big sticks back then and they'd use 'em. Quick!

"They'd let you stand like that for a while and then they would take you into the Deputy's Office. He'd be sitting down at his big desk in front of you. You'd be standing in front of him with the guards around you. He'd ask you why you done whatever they say you did. You'd say your piece and then he'd tell you what he was going to do with you.

"At that time there was four places they could send you if they wanted to punish you. One place was the punishment block where they put all of the real bad troublemakers. Men that was always fighting or getting into some kind of trouble. They'd keep a man in the punishment block for a long time. They put him there years before they let him out. It was a whole separate block where everyone stayed locked in their cell. They never came out. No commissary or nothing. They might let them have a smoke every once in a while and they'd feed them three full meals a day, but they didn't get much more.

"Another place was the Gallery which was the top range of one of the blocks. It was just like the punishment block except they'd only keep a man up there for no more than a year. Usually a few months or so.

"Then there was what they called the Klondike. It was the back part of one of the blocks. I was there a few times when I was at Eastern. They put me in a small cell and gave me half a thin blanket and I had to sleep on a steel bed with no mattress. There were no lights inside, but it wasn't cold. I got two slices of bread twice a day. There was a cold-water spigot in the cell so I had all the water I needed. Every 72 hours I got one full meal. I was in there a few times, but the most time I did in there was 15 days.

"Then there was what they called the Hole. I remember there was a guy they say cursed at the Deputy. They put him in the Hole for four days. Then they took him to the Deputy and they say he cursed at him again, so they put him back in the Hole for 30 days. When they took him to the Deputy again, they say he acted up again. But they figured he was crazy and so they just let him alone after that. The Hole was a four-by-four-by-four-foot cell with a solid door they kept shut. You couldn't stand up or lay down all the way. You'd get bread and water in there with a full meal every three days. No sir, that Hole was no joke."

Prison Today

"The food changed a lot. It got a lot better. When I first came to prison we ate everything out of one bowl. They didn't have no trays like they do now. We would go through the line with our bowl and utensils and they would put all the food into the bowl. Everything went into that bowl. It took me about 11 years before I got used to the food. But [in the Sixties] things got better, everything got better. You got chicken and beef. They didn't have none of that. . . .

"They treat you a lot better now. They have better medical care with real doctors and nurses. Inmates used to do all that. They have medication. I remember all they would give you was Epsom Salts for everything. They have college and schools now with teachers.

They didn't have none of that. . . . It's a lot better now. It's more human. . . .

"What makes me happy? Truthfully? If I could get a couple of Snickers Bars tonight and go to bed full and not hungry—I'm happy. Before they let you buy commissary in prison, I used to go to sleep hungry. Now with commissary and the 18 cents an hour I make, I'm happy. . . .

"At the present time I'm content. One thing, I have no worries. If I were in the streets, I'd worry about getting robbed, going here and there, getting beat up. Here I don't worry. Here I can lock my cell and nobody bothers me."

The Prison System

"Nobody owes me anything except the correctional system. They took 40 years of my life. . . . Prisons don't correct anything. People can go to college in here and get a degree but they can't get a job. What chance does anyone have without a job? Most of these guys just need a job. That's all. Create jobs, and 75 percent of these people wouldn't be in prison. . . . People don't need rehabilitation. They need to let inmates teach each other so everybody gets a trade. They need to have jobs to send these guys to. . . .

"The system creates crime. The angry people in prison are poor black guys. Where do you think they got the stuff to sell? Some white guy gave it to them. . . .

"I prefer capital punishment than leaving a man on death row for five, six, seven years. That's cruel. That may not be unusual but it's cruel. . . .

"The purpose of prison is to bring you to your senses and let you know you can't go against society and get away with it. The rule of law. You need the rule of law. . . .

"I don't think there will be anything good coming out of this interview."

Mr. Brown refuses to apply for parole, even though he has been eligible for many years. He has decided to remain a permanent resident of the Department of Corrections. Ironically, the cruelest thing the prison system could do to this man would be to release him to a society that he can no longer survive.

There are many more people like Mr. Brown in institutions throughout the country: spiritless, frightened souls who are quietly waiting to die in the only environment they feel comfortable in. These people represent a growing underclass of dependents in a world of change.

If this doesn't disturb you, maybe it should. Our system has become expert at making people forget about ever being free. If that doesn't bother you, then Mr. Brown wishes to thank you for being generous enough to pay the twenty- to thirty-thousand dollars a year it takes to keep him where he wants to be.

Chapter 12

Interview With Jacko: Surviving the Hole

Editor's Note

In 1840, the superintendent of the Norfolk Island penal colony, Alexander Maconochie, invented a system of "grades" that still enjoys wide use in American prisons. A typical system uses three grades. For any serious infraction, a prisoner is sentenced to solitary confinement for 30 days, with the first days spent in third-grade solitary—"the Hole." The solid door of the Hole closes out all light and sound. Meals consist of two slices of bread per day and water, with a full meal every third day. After six days of good behavior, the prisoner graduates to second-grade solitary, where the barred door provides light and sound; three full meals are served daily, but no smoking or reading materials are allowed. After nine days of good behavior, the prisoner is then given first-grade solitary, where he has full access to smoking and reading materials. After 15 days of good behavior, the prisoner may be released back into the general population.

Hassine begins his interview of Jacko with a short description of the Pennsylvania system. What both refer to as the Hole is actually first-grade solitary confinement. Pennsylvania no longer allows the use of third- or second-grade solitary confinement. Does this make the Pennsylvania system any more humane than the graded systems used in other states? Arguing that all pain is relative, Hassine sees little difference among the systems. The following interview demonstrates this point.

While prison is punishment for those who have violated society's laws, the Hole is punishment for those who have

99

violated a prison's rules. The Hole represents a penal institution's harshest form of legalized punishment short of the death penalty. On the one hand, a prison always feeds an inmate to keep him strong and healthy; on the other, it develops and imposes new and more creative forms of punishment that seem to defy all standards of human decency.

When Mr. Brown recalled the Hole between the years of 1945 and 1955, he was describing the beginning of a twisted path which found its way to me some 35 years later. While the nature of punishment in prison seems to have changed, its intensity certainly has not.

In the 1950s, the Governor of Pennsylvania assigned the new Commissioner of Corrections the task of reforming the prison system. One of the things the new Commissioner changed was the way inmates were punished. The four-by-four-by-four-foot punishment cell described by Mr. Brown could no longer be used. Furthermore, it was required that inmates in solitary confinement be given three full meals per day and allowed exercise periods out of their cell. Corporal punishment was prohibited.

These profound changes generated a lot of resentment from prison employees, who felt unruly inmates were not being adequately punished. In response, what solitary confinement lost in severity it gained in total confinement time. Inmates who broke the rules were now sent to the Hole for much longer periods of time—in many cases, years at a time.

Other changes required that lights be provided for the men confined in solitary. In response to that, guards left bright, glaring lights shining in these isolated cells for 24 hours a day. One prison went so far as to build a cell out of transparent plexiglass, known as the "glass cage," in which unyieldingly bright lights glared down upon the exposed inmate.

Bright lights and more time were not the end to the backlash of post-reform punishments. Whenever possible, the cells in solitary were kept either shivering cold in the winter or stifling hot in the summer. Those three full meals a day were often served cold and in the most cruel manner. And, while corporal punishment was prohibited, "goon squads" were formed by the guards to administer unofficial physical punishment. These goon squads were often comprised of guards who were not assigned to the general population, so inmates could not recognize them. They never wore name tags and their activities were never reported, at least not by the staff.

Thus, despite all the reforms, deprivation and physical force remained the peacemaker at Graterford and other Pennsylvania prisons. While it was true that inmates in solitary were now fed three meals per day, given exercise time, and lights in their cell, the degree of cruelty remained the same or was more severe than it had been in the past.

In fact, conditions in the punishment units of Pennsylvania's prisons became such an outrage that in 1973 the Bureau of Corrections was faced with a court-ordered Consent Decree resulting from a class-action suit, *Incarcerated Citizens Union (ICU) v. Shapp*, filed in Federal District Court to challenge conditions in the state's solitary-confinement cells. The Court had decided to try to institute and enforce the reforms that the first Commissioner had attempted in the 1950s. The ICU Consent Decree once again significantly changed the way Pennsylvania punished its inmates.

In this interview with a fellow inmate, Jacko describes the Hole at Graterford from 1976 to 1978. He recalls a much different place than Mr. Brown's Klondike at Old Eastern Penitentiary.

"I stayed in the Hole back then and, to tell you the truth, it wasn't really too bad. They would call you over to the Day Captain's Office and give you a misconduct report. Then you would go about your business. Unless it was a real serious misconduct, like hitting a guard or something, they never locked a man up until after the misconduct hearing.

"A few days later you would get a pass to the old phone room which was off of the main corridor right across from the laundry. There was always a lot of people sitting on the benches in the waiting room of the Hearing Room who were waiting for their hearing. The room was small and stayed hot because there were no windows and a whole lot of people. You'd sit there for hours sometimes until a guard from the Hearing Room would come out and call your number.

"Once you finally got inside the Hearing Room, a guard would pat you down and tell you to sit down in a chair that was right in front of a big table. Sitting on the other side of the table was the Major, a counselor, and a work supervisor. If the Major wasn't there, it would be a Captain or another white shirt [officer]. One of them would read the misconduct to you and ask you how you wanted to plead.

"At this time, you got a chance to say whatever you wanted to and then the guard would ask you to step outside. You always got found guilty, so basically all you were doing was waiting to see what punishment they were going to give you. You'd sit in the waiting room for a little while more until the guard would call you back in the Hearing Room. He would pat you down again and make you sit down in the same chair. Then the Major or one of the other guys would tell you what you got.

"They didn't really have cell restriction, loss of privileges, or any of that stuff back then. If they didn't send you to the Hole, they put you on probation or put you on the Gallery. Probation was when they would warn you that, if you got another misconduct any time soon, you would go to the Hole. That was it.

"The Gallery was the back half [50 cells] of the top range of B-Block on the A-Block side. If they sent you there, you went right from the hearing. But once you got to your cell in the Gallery, you could give the guard a list of things that he would bring to you from your cell. You could even have a TV and radio in the Gallery, and you also got commissary once a week.

"The section of B-Block where the Gallery was at had a steel mesh screen running along the outside of the top tier walkway, which separated it from the rest of the block. But you could still see and holler down to your friends in general population on B-Block. It got pretty noisy at times, but the guards didn't really mess with you about that. For recreation, you went to a small yard area between A- and B-Block two hours a day and they brought food to you off the main line three times a day.

"If you went to the Hole, you went right to Siberia. That was a whole separate building out by the wall on the opposite side of the cell blocks. The official name was the Behavioral Adjustment Unit [BAU]. We'd call it Bad Actors University.

"When you went to Siberia, you didn't take anything with you. You got the same meals and yard time as in the Gallery, but that was about it. Plus the guards kept it real cold in there. And if you made a lot of noise, they'd tell you to be quiet. If you didn't stop, the goon squad rushed you and beat your ass. That kept things pretty quiet.

"But to tell you the truth, I didn't mind the Hole, because they would give me all the medication I asked for. I mean I got Valium and Darvons—all I wanted. I stayed high. And as long as you didn't mess with the guards, they pretty much left you alone. But it was cold."

In addition to the improved conditions in what was now called "Punitive Segregation," Jacko was afforded the right to appeal his misconduct to a Program Review Committee and then to the Superintendent. If the Superintendent would not give him the relief he asked for, he could take his appeal up to the Commissioner. When Mr. Brown went to the Hole decades before, however, all he could do was his time.

The ICU Consent Decree also brought about a limit to the amount of time a Hearing Committee could confine a man in Punitive Segregation: a maximum of 180 days in the BAU or Gallery for every misconduct report. In response to this, guards who had previously listed all of an inmate's infractions on one misconduct report now issued separate misconduct reports for every infraction. In this way, the Hearing Committee could continue its practice of sending troublemakers to the Hole for years at a time.

This rush to fill the Hole with long-term residents resulted in a long-term shortage of cells in the Gallery and BAU (now renamed the "Restrictive Housing Unit," or RHU). By the time I faced my first misconduct hearing in 1982 for the hamburger caper, the Gallery had been expanded to double its former capacity. Furthermore, part of the RHU was double-celled, so that solitary confinement at Graterford was not so solitary anymore.

Aggravating the problem was the violence at Graterford, which had caused a dramatic increase in the number of inmates seeking protective custody, or self-lockup. For a multitude of reasons, these men could not be protected in general population, so they chose to live in the safety of solitary confinement. By housing them on the Gallery, the prison administration imposed on them the same restrictions used for many of the men who were serving punitive-segregation time. Unfortunately, as the violence escalated, these restrictions were not enough to stem the tide of inmates seeking protective custody.

Consequently, the Hearing Committee was no longer free to punish misbehaving inmates by sending them to the RHU or the Gallery. There just weren't enough cells. So new sanctions were developed, one of which was the cell restriction I received for my burger infraction. Another was "double lock feed-in," which allowed an inmate to serve RHU time in his cell until such time as a cell in the RHU or the Gallery became available.

The nature and effect of punishment at Graterford are still in flux. In my view, guards' resistance to reform, combined with overcrowding, has to this day prevented a reasonable system of punishment from being realized or evaluated. Crisis management, along with a heavy dose of resentment and spite, still takes precedence over fair punishment.

PART III

Op Ed

Editor's Note

In this third section, Hassine presents several opinion essays which express his social-activist view of the prison system. Unlike the material presented in the first two sections, each of these op ed chapters are intended to argue a point. Whether readers agree or disagree with any of these arguments, the author's point of view is once again an authentic perspective on some of the most pressing problems facing American prisons today.

Chapter 13

Prison Overcrowding

Editor's Note

Not long ago, criminologists debated whether society has a natural "capacity to punish." Interest in this question was motivated by the observation that while crime rates rise and fall over time, imprisonment rates have remained constant throughout history. But in the late 1970s, however, imprisonment rates began to explode, refuting the empirical basis of this debate. While the causes of the population explosion are clear, the effects are yet to be discovered. When the full effects of overcrowding are finally examined, however, the effects on the quality of prison life will more than likely be excluded. For that reason alone, the author's accounting of these effects are of tantamount importance.

What Is Overcrowding?

Prison overcrowding is a much overused term to describe an aggregate of related conditions that plague prisons all over the country. Despite its overuse, it is seldom explained in graphic terms that students and lay people can fully grasp. Instead, it is depicted as a vague, generalized "social problem"—a euphemism for the extreme, hopeless, horrifying, and tragic conditions that truly exist. The blood and guts of what prison overcrowding is *inside* and what it really does to the insiders remains an enigma to most outsiders.

The thin but durable veneer of this euphemism was poignantly revealed to me by a fellow inmate as we sat on the crowded bleachers of a crowded yard in a very overcrowded prison. After reading a newspaper article on the topic, he spat a plug of tobacco on the ground, turned to me, and said: "These people keep blaming everything in here on overcrowding. It's overcrowding this and overcrowding that. Well, who the hell *is* this guy that's overcrowding us, anyway? And, if they know he's causing all these problems, why the hell don't they lock his ass up?"

His comment, more than just an angry sarcasm, posed a fundamental question about something that many of those with only a reader's knowledge of prison life view simply as an eyesore in the Great American Landscape. What *is* prison overcrowding and what exactly does it do?

First Came Crowded

As the term implies, prisons must have been crowded before they became overcrowded. First some distinction must be made between the two conditions, one being that crowding in prisons was planned while overcrowding was not. Since the early 1800s when penitentiaries were first built, the one aspect of prison design that has survived is the practice of housing as many inmates as possible in the smallest cells possible, while meeting their minimal needs using a minimum of staff.

When I first came to Graterford, I entered a very crowded place supported by a very controlled, structured system designed to house a mass of inmates, yet provide for them in the most economical way. Years of prison riots, reform, trial and error, design innovations, common sense, and just plain luck have brought about an evolution of prisons into a system of 1700 men responding to klaxon bells, obeying orders, and traveling in unison down a tried and true maze of day-to-day prison existence.

Then Came Overcrowded

With the arrival of that "guy" who was overcrowding us, suddenly nothing worked right. Our lives became a daily challenge to avoid injury and stay out of trouble, which left us little time to reflect on the errors of our ways. In essence, the penitentiary evolved into a ghetto.

Once its prison population exceeded design capacity, Graterford became overcrowded. This numerical imbalance forced officials to institute double-celling or barracks-styled housing in order to accommodate the surplus population, despite the fact that the prison's cell blocks were not built for that kind of traffic.

While much can be argued about the psychological and physical dangers of squeezing two men into a poorly lit, poorly ventilated, bathroom-sized cell, the true evil of overcrowding has very little to do with crowded living space. Human beings, if they must, can and have lived in caves and tunnels. The destructive nature of prison overcrowding stems from the fact that it came unplanned and imposed on a system specifically created to discourage the confinement of too many inmates in one place.

Suddenly we inmates found ourselves at odds with our own rigidly designed environment. Furthermore, while inmate populations skyrocketed, the hiring of staff to support them did not increase proportionately. In Graterford and other prisons that I have been exposed to, the hiring of treatment staff (e.g., teachers, counselors, and vocational instructors) was in fact frozen—while an endless number of illiterate and needy inmates stormed the prison gates.

Overcrowding as a Personal Experience

As an inmate confined to one Pennsylvania prison or another since 1981, I have experienced what overcrowding has done, is doing, and threatens to do. By the mid-1980s, I was fairly well dug into my prison routine, working, obeying, and vegetating. I had a single cell, and for better or worse the prison system was functioning at an adequate level.

Then one day, my cell door opened and another man was shoved inside. Overcrowding had just introduced himself to me, and almost immediately it began to alter my world.

My first argument with my new co-tenant was, of course, over who got the top or bottom bunk. Then we fought over lights on or lights off, hygiene habits, toilet-use etiquette, cell cleaning, property storage, and whose friends could visit. Then there was missing property, accusations of thievery, snoring, farting, and smoking. As these arguments raged on every day, new ones would arise to make things worse.

Since the prison staff was somewhat taken by surprise by this sudden overpopulation, there was no time to plan or screen double-celling. Inmates were shoved together solely on the basis of race, age, or cell availability. Nor did an inmate have any opportunity to screen potential cellmates. If you didn't voluntarily find someone to move in with you, one would be picked for you at random. This practice contributed significantly to the prison population's incompatibility with double-celling. It was bad enough living with a stranger in such close quarters without having to worry about whether he was a Jeffrey Dahmer.

As my day-to-day struggle with my cellmate became a fact of life, I realized how much this guy Mr. Overcrowding was causing me more serious problems in every aspect of my prison life. As the next chapter shows, the possibility of one day waking up to a cannibal beside me, while certainly a cause for alarm, proved to be the least of my concerns.

Chapter 14

Homosexuality: The Pink Cells

Editor's Note

Prison sexuality is not a traditional area of criminological research. Lacking both an adequate theory and longitudinal data, we cannot say whether homosexuality is more or less common in prisons today than it was in 1980, for example. According to the author, however, the problems associated with homosexuality in prison have increased steadily. His analysis of this trend points to four causes.

Overcrowding has drastically increased homosexual activity in prison. The reasons for this include: (1) double-celling, (2) societal tolerance, (3) an increase in youthful offenders, and (4) understaffing.

Double-Celling

When two strangers are crammed randomly together into a small cell, something very primitive occurs: the stronger inmate dominates the weaker one. If the stronger happens to be an aggressive homosexual or has been a victim of rape, then there is a very good chance that the weaker will be raped by the stronger.

This is not a matter of homosexuality as an alternate lifestyle. The type of homosexual conduct I'm referring to is the vilest, most degrading form of violence one man can inflict upon another. It is not an expression of love, caring, or even passion. Prison rape is the way by which one man can dominate another for the sole purpose of establishing power and absolute control over his victim. It can also lead to prostitution, beatings, and any other conceivable form of degradation. Today, double-celling is considered to be the greatest cause for the proliferation of prison rape.

Most victims of rape in prison do not report it because of the consequences. They worry not only about reprisals but also about exposing their humiliation to other inmates. If a victim reports the incident, he will be locked in the Hole indefinitely for his own protection and pressured to testify against the rapist. This means paperwork in his files, possibly even a published court decision graphically detailing his ordeal. The preferred option is to grin and bear it rather than have one's reputation dragged through the mud.

The spread of rape and homosexuality in overcrowded prisons also creates problems that are unique to double-celled prison environments. For example, if an inmate is assigned a homosexual to double cell with, there is a greater likelihood that his cell will be burglarized. Homosexuals in prisons are perceived as weak men who cannot defend themselves, so their cells tend to be more likely targets for thieves and predatory inmates.

Then there is the problem of perception. An inmate assigned a homosexual "cellee" will have to deal with everyone who thinks he is having sex with his cohabitant. This in turn will subject him to the ill intentions of thieves and rapists seeking to test his character. Also, an inmate can eventually expect to walk in while his cellmate is having sex with another inmate. This is a serious breach in prison etiquette and often leads to violence between cellees.

Societal Tolerance

Clearly things have changed in the way society views homosexuality. This greater tolerance and acceptance of individual sexual preferences has also found its way into prisons. Statistically, there is always a certain percentage of prison guards and administrators who are homosexual. Comedian Lenny Bruce once pointed out that sending a gay man to an all-male prison was in fact a reward, not a punishment. Taking this scenario a step further, prison is an ideal place for a homosexual not only as an inmate but also as a guard.

Over the past 14 years, I have met professed homosexuals at virtually every level of the prison bureaucracy. I have been shown love letters from staff to their inmate lovers, and vice versa. A chaplain at Western Penitentiary was fired after being caught having sex with an inmate in the prison chapel.

In a prison setting, the tolerance of homosexual conduct between inmates and staff creates the likelihood of favoritism toward these inmates. Sometimes these sexual relationships can lead to blackmail or the smuggling of contraband. Even more harmful is the jealousy and resentment that such favoritism fosters, resulting in a greater loss of respect for the prison administration.

It is little wonder that some homosexuals have achieved a high status in the prison hierarchy, because administrators feel less threatened by them and therefore offer them more privileges and favors than others. The majority population of heterosexuals, meanwhile, is forced to tolerate these men in high places, which only provokes more anger and envy.

There are many theories about why this has happened, one being that the administration is promoting homosexuality because they realize that a sexually satisfied inmate is a less troublesome one. Another theory holds that, since homosexuals are presumed to be fundamentally weak, they are more likely to become informants and thereby receive more privileges. Yet another theory simply states that, since it is now acceptable to be gay in prison, men are just enjoying themselves while they can. Whatever the reasons, homosexuals have become major players in prison populations.

It is frustrating enough that only homosexual inmates can enjoy sex in prison, but their added privileges have fueled speculation that the prison administration has lost its ability to be fair. As long as the heterosexual prison population is forced to endure administratively sanctioned homosexuality while being denied their own conjugal rights, tensions between homosexual and heterosexual inmates will continue to mount.

A vivid example of the unfairness of the situation is the prison system's policy toward visitations. An inmate can be issued a misconduct for kissing and hugging his wife in the visiting room. As a result, he may be given 60 days in the Hole and lose his visitation rights for at least a year. But if two men are caught kissing or hugging each other in the prison population, though an infraction of the rules, such displays of affection are generally tolerated. I know of no misconducts that have ever been issued for such activity. This disparity in punishment raises the question of whether prisons should in all fairness allow heterosexual conjugal visits and privileges.

Increase in Youthful Offenders

When I first entered the prison system at age 25, I was considered a relatively young inmate. This would not be the case today since the dramatic increase in the number of teenage inmates in adult prisons. My current cellmate has been serving a life sentence in an adult facility since he was 14, and I personally know a dozen or more men who were 16 when they first came to prison.

Teenage inmates are generally weaker and more frightened than their older counterparts. This means that they are more likely to be the object of interest to predatory inmates looking to extort and/or rape them. Given the unstable, hostile conditions of overcrowded prisons, most teenage inmates do in fact become victims, and that victimization usually begins or ends in rape.

In *Against Our Will: Men, Women, and Rape*,[1] author Susan Brownmiller included a study entitled "Sexual Assaults in the Philadelphia Prison System" by Assistant District Attorney Alan J. Davis. The study concluded that "virtually every slightly built young man committed by the courts is sexually approached within a day or two after admission to prison. Many of these young men are repeatedly raped by gangs of inmates. Others, because of the threat of gang rape, seek protection by entering into a homosexual relationship with an individual tormentor. . . . Only the tougher and more hardened young men, and those few so obviously frail that they are immediately locked up for their own protection, escape homosexual rape." Brownmiller summarizes: "Homosexual assault, this district attorney learned, had become an extra form of punishment that was part and parcel of imprisonment, a punishment never intended by the sentence of the court."

If teenagers are anything, they are resilient. When a young felon gets raped and victimized, he overcomes the trauma by incorporating his violation into part of his lifestyle. If you can't beat 'em, they reason,

1. Reference : Brownmiller, Susan (1975) 1993. *Against Our Will*. New York, NY: Fawcett.

join 'em. So these young victims tend to go out and find victims of their own in order to regain some of the respect they feel they have lost. This practice creates a cycle of victimization of and by youth, thereby proliferating the practice of violent homosexuality.

Double-celling renders it impossible to control this phenomenon in today's prisons. Hence, society will have to deal with the yet undetermined consequences of so many brutally traumatized inmates lost in our prisons and eventually on our streets.

Understaffing

The conclusion that prison understaffing, combined with random double-celling, results in less supervision and more forbidden conduct is obvious. But there are other ways understaffing affects homosexuality.

With more guards on overtime, the security force tends to follow the path of least resistance. For example, when TV sets were first allowed in individual cells, most guards objected that they rendered prison life too comfortable and therefore were unacceptable. However, with the advent of overcrowding, seldom will you find a guard who does not condone a TV in a cell; it simply encourages more cell time by inmates, less work for staff, and less violence. Likewise, the same reasoning seems to apply to homosexuality in inmates' cells. Two lovers in a cell with a TV will find very little reason to leave their cell.

Most guards tacitly approve the practice of homosexuality, giving new meaning to the proverb, "Love conquers all." This policy has often backfired, however, since one of the most common causes of violence in prisons are inmate love triangles and lovers' quarrels, which can lead to murder, maiming, savage beatings, and revenge by the willful infection of AIDS.

Homosexuality in overcrowded prisons may solve some short-term problems, but it lays the groundwork for long-term consequences. Encouraging involuntary homosexuality on a large segment of the prison population ultimately leads to (1) more violence between inmates, (2) the proliferation of diseases, (3) the spread of sexual dysfunction, and (4) more hatred for the system which promotes this practice.

As convicts re-enter the outside world and take with them their learned prison behavior, the conduct that has destabilized prisons will threaten to destabilize society. The role prisons play in encouraging this change in sexual orientation, particularly the psychological effect on its raped youth, is something that demands serious examination—before short-term prison gains become a long-term nightmare for society.

Chapter 15

Relationships Between Inmates and Guards

Editor's Note

Prisoners and their keepers have little in common. Yet as the author notes, the routine personal relationships between prisoners and guards constitute an important component of the larger social system within prisons. His analysis of these relationships highlights the importance of socializing neophyte staff.

When I first entered prison, I was surprised to discover that there was no open hostility between guards and inmates. As a matter of fact, many inmates and guards went out of their way to establish relationships with each other. Inmates befriended guards in the hope that they would get such benefits as an extra phone call, special shower time, or the overlooking of some minor infraction. In turn, guards encouraged friendly relations with inmates because they wanted to get information or just to keep the peace and make it through another day without getting hurt.

From what I have observed, most guards who have been attacked were attempting to enforce some petty rule. Over time, guards have learned that it doesn't always pay to be too rigid about prison regulations. Thus, an unwritten agreement has been established between inmates and guards: inmates get what they want by being friendly and nonaggressive, while guards ensure their own safety by not strictly enforcing the rules. For the most part, inmates

manipulate the guards' desire for safety, and guards exploit the inmates' need for autonomy.

By the mid-1980s, things changed with overcrowding and the
influx of new prison subcultures. Administrators could not hire new
guards fast enough to keep pace with the flood of inmates, so the
practice of overtime was employed. Any guard who was willing to
work overtime could get it, with the result that on any given day a
large percentage of guards were on overtime. This phenomenon had
the immediate impact of introducing many exhausted, irritable
guards into the work force, often on shifts with which they were not
familiar.

The combination of these two factors virtually destroyed all
sense of continuity and uniform treatment that the prison had established over the years. The most important element needed to
maintain a workable relationship between inmates and staff is a
continuity of treatment. Disturb the inmates' expectation of that
continuity, and you destroy the delicate balance between them and
the staff. This lays the groundwork for a riot.

A tired, overworked guard on an unfamiliar shift tends to be
unwilling to offer any assistance. Being a stranger to the unique
inmate hierarchy of his newly assigned unit, he is unable to conform
to longstanding customs and practices. This often spells disaster, as
once workable relations between keeper and kept deteriorate into
anger, distrust, and hatred. It has been my experience that this breakdown in relations inevitably provokes an upsurge of violence, disorder, and rioting.

There is an even more insidious consequence of excessive overtime that undermines inmate and guard relationships. In every
prison there is a percentage of guards who are so rigid and unpopu-
lar with inmates, or so incompetent, that they are given work as-
signments that keep them away from contact with prisoners, such
as tower duty or the late-night shift. Any prison administrator of
intelligence knows that these kinds of guards can jeopardize the
tenuous order and operation of a prison. With the advent of unlim-
ited overtime, however, these guards have found their way into the
prison mainstream. As expected, their presence has further exacer-
bated an already tense and uncertain environment.

The overexposure of tired, irritable, overworked, and sometimes
inexperienced and antagonistic guards to the population has created

an inconsistent and unpredictable prison environment, especially because guards know much less about what inmates are thinking, and vice versa. With all the new inmates coming in and out of prisons every year, it is becoming increasingly difficult for the staff to keep track of who is who and who is doing what, and even harder for a prison security force trying to employ traditional investigative and intelligence methods. In the old days, everyone knew each other in a prison and knew pretty well what everyone else was up to. Not so today.

The only way the security system can effectively operate in a prison today is by soliciting the services of inmate informants, or "snitches." Guards maintain a legion of snitches and openly advertise that fact to the inmate population. In order to keep their informants in force, prison administrators have gone overboard to reward and protect them. Their rationale is that every informant constitutes an unpaid member of the security force that helps to compensate for understaffing. This almost exclusive reliance on informants for information and intelligence creates several conditions, including:

1. Keeping the inmate population at odds with each other over who is the informant in their midst.

2. Elevating snitches in the prison hierarchy, since they are often rewarded with the best jobs, highest pay, and best living conditions.

3. Increasing the growing antagonism between long-term inmates and parole violators, who are more likely to become informants in order to gain early parole and relative comfort during their brief stay in prison.

4. A proliferation of drugs entering the prison, as informants act as conduits for drug smuggling in order to attract their targets.

5. Providing prison administrators with unrealistic perceptions of inmate activity, as informants become less credible the more they are used.

This last condition often occurs because an informant is pursuing his own interests and therefore will only inform on those activities that do not affect his particular business. Such self-serving information is only as accurate as the informant needs it to be. Sometimes it is a fabricated reflection of what he knows the administration wants to hear. Thus, many informants provide the kind of information that subordinates the truth in order to conform to a pre-existing view.

To use a classic example of this, I knew an ambitious guard in 1983 who told me he used his overtime to ensure himself a more substantial pension benefit. (In those days, pensions were based on the three highest annual salaries rather than on base salary.) So he worked double shifts seven days a week for three years. But as a result, he became useless. He was either too listless and irritable or falling asleep all the time. In order to convince his superiors of his efficiency, he would reward informants who gave him information that he could use to issue misconducts. Consequently, his informants were in turn able to operate a massive drug and homosexual prostitution ring under his protection. Administrators ended up buying a nickel's worth of information for $1,000's worth of corruption.

Another example involved a prison murder. One day in the yard, two inmates fought over drugs until one of them was stabbed to death in plain view of dozens of witnesses. Subsequently, the prison security officer received numerous notes from inmates wishing to give eyewitness accounts. This enabled the authorities to quickly identify the culprit. But the informants all gave self-serving details of the crime and its motives, until there were so many contradicting versions of what happened that all their testimony was rendered worthless. Without enough evidence, the state was forced to offer the murderer five to ten years in return for a guilty plea. Such a sentence for a murder committed in a public prison yard is so lenient that it could be considered a license to kill. This failure of justice on the part of the prison administration was precipitated by its exclusive reliance on prejudiced informants.

The end result is that today's prisons have become even more violent. Inmates do not trust each other, because informants call the shots and even initiate or encourage most of the crimes they report. Guards are overworked and increasingly alienated from the mainstream of prison life. And finally, a new breed of young, violent, ignorant, drug-addicted, and completely self-absorbed criminals is pouring in and leaving even the most veteran inmates and staff scared to death.

Chapter 16

A Theory of Prison Evolution

Editor's Note

The author's view of prison adaptation, or evolution, attributes the recent breakdown of American prisons to overcrowding. In simplest terms, each prison has a natural population capacity, based on its design, infrastructure, and resources. When the prison's natural capacity is exceeded, it is launched into an unpredictable trajectory. Hassine illustrates this theory with the example of Graterford.

At a recent group-counseling session I heard someone say that the problem with prisons today is that they no longer have any direction. That statement hit me like a lock in a sock, as I came to a realization: Graterford had no direction, so the gangs, thieves, extortionists, and the walls themselves provided direction in the only way they could—through greed and brutality.

In the early and mid-1980s, Graterford was a prison that maintained control by establishing *no* controls. The only rule that was strictly applied was "Don't try to escape," and the walls made this easy to enforce. Everything else was up for grabs. Ironically, this anarchic style of prison management was fairly effective. Inmates spent so much time protecting themselves from each other that few had the opportunity to even consider escape. Additionally, the high rate of inmate murders and death by drug overdose ultimately maintained the prison society's own form of population control.

If there is any lesson to be learned from Graterford, it is in the *evolution* of prisons: how factors in a prison's design, management, structure, and inmate population can work with and against each other in its transition from a prison to a tribe of gangs to a kingdom of inmates.

To better understand some of the underlying factors, we should consider the original design concept of Graterford itself. It would be safe to say that the prison's builders followed the principle that a larger prison is a better prison; hence its five mammoth cell blocks and its gigantic walls. But an unforseen factor ultimately crippled this bigger-is-better theory of prison design: the huge cost it would take to supervise the 2,144 inmates Graterford was originally intended to hold. With the advent of the Great Depression and World War II, spending a fortune to maintain an oversized prison colony grew less and less practical.

For four decades, the inmate population at Graterford remained manageably small and well below capacity, so the prison's design had yet to be tested. Its only serious drawbacks at the time were the obvious conditions of too little manpower to supervise too many inmates and the extraordinary length of the blocks that made visual observation difficult. The inmate population surge of the 1970s changed all that, causing the inherent failure of Graterford's design to become alarmingly apparent: bigger was *not* better.

It is my contention that the growth of a prison population beyond 1,500 inmates is most likely to trigger a prison's process of degenerative evolution. That threshold figure can be much lower if the prison is grossly understaffed and/or mismanaged. Generally, the faster an inmate population grows beyond 1,500, the more unpredictable that population becomes.

The struggle for control over a prison can be likened to a game of chess: whoever maintains control of the center of the board is likely to dominate the whole board and win the game. If the center in this analogy is the greater mass of an inmate population, then an administration must control its movement and conduct in order to maintain control of the prison. The biggest concerns for management are the fringes of the population outside the center: convicts who are unresponsive to any form of control or imposed discipline, including prison gang leaders, rapists, rabble-rousers, sociopaths, and prison assassins.

The chief factor for control of a prison's center is the protection of the inmate population. Inmates in general will follow the path perceived to be the safest. To control the center, the administration has to keep the fringes from creating so much fear and disorder that inmates move outside the center to find safety, which can happen spontaneously and unpredictably.

As the inmate center grows in size, so too does the inmate fringe. Once the number of inmates outside the center becomes so great that groups and sub-groups begin to form, their ability to adversely influence conditions in the center will increase dramatically. Consequently, the administration will need more manpower and financial resources to maintain a safe and orderly environment at the center. Even with sufficient funds and staffing, a prison administration will be hard pressed to overcome the destabilizing effects of such powerful fringe elements as they consolidate their forces. If management cannot meet all the needs of the expanding inmate center, then its control of that center becomes weaker, while the destructive power of the inmate fringe grows stronger.

If the general population grows so rapidly that the prison staff can no longer protect those in the center, small, secure groups will form until the whole prison population becomes a collection of fringe groups seeking protection. The administration's control will then be limited to only basic physical confinement.

At this point, the prison has evolved into a collective tribe made up of clans working independently of and at odds with each other. Now anything can happen, as the fringe groups further explore the limits of their power and the prison administration responds with more desperate measures to regain control. While the staff may still control some parts of the center, its authority is so undermined that it is treated as just another clan.

During this tribal stage, the inmate population becomes extremely sensitive to changes in its composition. For example, as more violent or drug-addicted inmates enter the system, their potential to destabilize the prison skyrockets as the weakened prison administration's ability to neutralize them plummets.

Once the mounting chaos within the prison population begins to crystallize into a common identity and self-awareness on the part of the inmates, the prison will evolve into a kingdom. Clans will work together to ensure that the administration can never re-establish control of the center. While these clans will continue to challenge each other for dominance, no one clan can ever muster enough resources to maintain total control.

Graterford serves as a fitting example of an evolving prison. During the 1970s, its inmate population increased so rapidly in inverse proportion to decreasing staff and funding that its evolution was inevitable. At that time, a growing number of gang members flooded into Graterford as the result of a surge of gang wars in Philadelphia. In 1969, Eastern Penitentiary was shut down and a large number of inner-city African-American inmates wound up in Graterford. These conditions only served to accelerate Graterford's entry into the tribal stage.

When I arrived at Graterford in 1981, the population was at an all-time high of 1,800 and the administration had already lost control over its epidemic of violence. As described earlier by Double D, it apparently made one last attempt to establish control of the center by empowering Rocky and his gang to neutralize the activities of the fringe. But when the clans united to run Rocky out of the prison, the administration not only lost more control, but the Kingdom of Inmates learned the effectiveness of organization.

Chicken Sunday marked the final stage of Graterford's evolution into a kingdom, when inmates realized for the first time that *they*, and not the staff, controlled the space within its concrete walls. Hence, they joined forces to protect their interests against the administration's and defend the underground economy.

As I look back on the failure of Graterford as a system of social engineering, I remember how quickly guards and inmates alike retrogressed from order to anarchy. I realize now that the consequences of such a failed social system *outside* these walls could be even more terrifying. Civilization can be as fragile as our freedom, and the same men who today stand for all that is good in the world can tomorrow turn into savage barbarians who exploit the weak.

Graterford remains to this day a harsh reminder of how a dense concentration of men left to fend for themselves can create a Darwinian tidal pool of lifeforms perfected by hardships—an evolutionary process that ensures the survival of only the strongest and the most resourceful.

Chapter 17

Conclusion: The Runaway Train

Editor's Note

The author's analogy here suggests that the problems facing American prisons will lead inevitably to cataclysm. Impending doom has been a constant theme of American prisons and prison reform movements. For nearly three centuries, American prisons have confronted one crisis after another and, surviving each one, have gone relatively unchanged. To be sure, many of the system components that we take for granted today—probation, parole, etc.—are products of these crises. In this light, the author point outs correctly that the challenges facing American prisons today are potentially more cataclysmic than any past crisis.

Overcrowding is the harbinger of cataclysmic change in our nation's prison system. That change is so profound that it is transforming the very structure and operation of the entire system, not just individual prisons. On the one hand, it is giving birth to a renegade bureaucracy obsessed with maintaining its own uncertain existence in the struggle to retain control over the penal system. On the other hand, it is creating a terrified population of inmates who have lost all sense of security and live like "moment dwellers" with no thought of the future.

To better understand the nature and extent of this transformation, consider the analogy of a runaway train. Imagine you're standing on the boarding platform of a train station. As you wait, you take for granted that your train will come to take you to your destination. Experience has led you to rely on this train as an efficient means of mass transit.

Your train finally arrives. You step aboard and take your seat among a carload of other commuters. As the train travels along, you sense that it's moving faster than usual. This does not alarm you, but you stop reading your newspaper, take a look at your watch, then peer out a window. You notice the countryside whizzing past you at an increasing rate. Suddenly you see the train speed past the station where you were supposed to get off.

Now you are alarmed. But a voice over the loudspeaker apologizes for the inconvenience, assures everyone that everything is under control, and promises the train will stop at the next station. The train continues to accelerate.

Soon, the train hurtles past yet another station. You begin to realize that something is seriously wrong. You try to find a conductor or anyone in authority, but you get caught in a crush of passengers who have decided to do the same thing. Again you hear the loudspeaker voice, but because of all the confusion you can't make out what it is saying. In any event, you no longer trust any announcements. The train plunges forward out of control, faster and faster.

The crowd, the uncertainty, and the noise causes a panic. It is at this point that the train has been transformed from a vehicle of mass transit to a machine that generates fear, panic, and anger among passengers who now must face an uncertain future.

As panic and confusion rise, desperation sets in. No one cares anymore about their jobs, their schedules, or their futures. Everyone is thinking about right now and how they are going to survive this madness. Every human intuition has surrendered to the primitive instincts of "survival of the fittest." The passengers are no longer passengers, and the train is no longer a train.

Such is the plight of a prison inmate.

Now imagine that you are the train engineer. You were the first to realize the train's acceleration problem. Because you are a trained expert, you felt certain you would be able to fix any mechanical problem. You radio the home office and inform them of the problem, then you pull out your repair manual and go about trying to fix the engine. But the train continues to accelerate and refuses to respond to any of your efforts. At this point you begin to worry.

As you work feverishly to control the train, you hear passengers banging on your engineer's door. The frustration of your failed efforts, the loud din of the uncooperative engine, and the panicking cries of passengers combine to unnerve you. You angrily take a moment to bark over the loudspeaker, "Everything is under control—please remain in your seats." But the screams and banging intensify as the train continues to accelerate beyond your control. You need help but you know you're not going to get any.

Despite your desperate and futile efforts, you realize that the longer you fail to slow your train, the more problems you'll be forced to fix. Weaknesses in design and construction of the train have caused additional mechanical failures. You find yourself reacting to a multitude of new emergencies that give you little or no opportunity to address the original problem. You know that unless this acceleration is stopped, collision or derailment is imminent.

At this point, you are no longer a trained professional concerned only with train schedules and engine maintenance. You have become a reactionary crisis-control manager who no longer cares where the train is headed. Your main goal now is to avert a catastrophe, and you have to keep those hysterical passengers from interfering with what you're trying to do. Meanwhile, the train races faster and faster.

Such is the dilemma of a prison's staff and its administration.

Now imagine that you are another commuter on a station platform, waiting for a train. All of a sudden you see your train speed past you. You catch a glimpse of passengers banging on the passing windows. You notice the hysteria on their faces and that some of them are holding up signs which you can't make out because the train is moving too fast, too out of control.

This causes you some concern until you hear an authoritative voice over a loudspeaker, apologizing for the inconvenience and announcing that everything is well under control. You are instructed to wait calmly for the next train which will arrive shortly.

Though annoyed, you are a bit relieved that you will at least be able to reach your destination. It never occurs to you that once you board the next train, the same thing that is happening to the hysterical, sign-waving passengers you just saw could also happen to you.

Such is the plight of the public at large.

The message of this parable is all too clear. I am one of those hysterical passengers on the runaway train, and this book is a sign that I'm waving at my window, hoping against hope that someone outside the train can read it and get help to us before a catastrophe destroys us all. Prison administrators are the frantic engineers trying to keep me and the other hysterical passengers out of their way while they work to bring the runaway train back under control.

And you, my readers, are the people calmly standing in the station as we tear by. You live in a normal world with all of its normal worries, such as whether your train will be on time or whether you will be late for work. A brief glimpse of our frantic faces may disturb your normal world for a moment.

Will you assume that everything is really all right and go back to reading your newspapers? Or will you to try to get help to those passengers who, in the final analysis, are fellow human beings on the train of life?

Afterword

Richard A. Wright
University of Scranton

Throughout the history of incarceration, countless prisoners have written books about their experiences behind bars. "Prose and cons" appear to go together like love and marriage, as articulate, curious inmates find the right mixture of spare time, exotic subject matter, and memorable characters to fill their notebooks. This is why writing courses and inmate newspapers and newsletters thrive in most prisons.

It should be no surprise, then, that penitentiaries have transformed aspiring writers into skilled essayists (see Abbott 1982; Jackson 1970) or even brilliant authors (see Genet [1949] 1964; Solzhenitsyn 1974, 1975, 1976). As a criminologist whose specialty is corrections, I have read numerous books written by prisoners. None offer more insight into the daily routines and everyday crises in contemporary American prisons than Victor Hassine's *Life Without Parole*.

For me, reading this book was like spending a few days meandering through the cellblocks of a men's maximum-security prison. Those familiar with these institutions will find the characters and situations described by Hassine credible and vivid. For students and lay persons, no rival work offers a superior, word-for-word introduction to modern prison life.

What follows are some reflections about how Hassine's book relates to certain larger issues in social research and the correctional literature, concluding with a few thoughts about the policy implications of *Life Without Parole*.

Victor Hassine, Graterford, and External Validity

Social scientists are always concerned about whether their observations are idiosyncratic or can be generalized to other persons,
settings, and situations. This is because researchers usually only
have sufficient resources to survey a handful among the throng of
individuals who share the particular characteristics they are interested in studying. In scientific jargon, this problem is known as
external validity: Is one's sample representative of some larger population (see Babbie 1992; Denzin 1989)?

External validity is a particularly serious problem in life-histo-
ries research, where one individual in one setting tries to speak for
many persons in different places (Denzin 1989). Although a number
of famous studies in criminology are life histories of one offender
(e.g., Shaw 1930; Sutherland 1937) or small groups of offenders (e.g.,
Ianni 1972; Whyte 1943), some scholars dismiss most examples of
these works as biased.

On the surface of things, the demand for external validity would
seem to pose insurmountable problems of interpretation in the cases
of Victor Hassine and Graterford. Hassine himself remarks that
when he first arrived at Graterford he was a "square john," prison
slang for a middle-class, law-abiding inmate who usually identifies
more with the staff than with other inmates. Few square johns end
up in maximum-security prisons, but most who do are murderers.
The square-john killer is a rare breed in maximum security, sharing
nothing more than an address with the lower-class career criminals
confined to the rest of the cellblock. Even more unusual, Hassine is
a Jewish immigrant from Egypt who has a law degree from a leading
American university. This combination of factors makes him a truly
unique prisoner.

Although the State Correctional Institution at Graterford is certainly more representative of American prisons than Victor Hassine
is of American prisoners, there are still problems in generalizing
from Graterford to other correctional settings. Graterford, which I
have toured along with many other correctional institutions
throughout the United States, is an infamous men's "big house"
penitentiary—the last stop for Pennsylvania's most dangerous male
felons. There are no other prisons like it in the state; for similarities,
one must consider such notorious institutions as Stateville Penitentiary in Illinois, Kansas State Penitentiary in Lansing, Huntsville

Prison in Texas, Washington State Penitentiary in Walla Walla, or the federal penitentiaries in Leavenworth, Kansas, and Atlanta, Georgia. Gangs, drugs, violence, and corruption are much more common in these penitentiaries than in other types of prisons that have fewer menacing inmates and custody complications.

In Graterford, Victor Hassine was a unique prisoner confined in an unusual setting. Normally, this combination would create an external validity nightmare. In *Life Without Parole*, however, Hassine writes more about fellow inmates in ordinary prison situations than about his own experiences at Graterford. This strategy converts a potential methodological catastrophe into a genuine success.

While Hassine and Graterford may be atypical, those familiar with prisons will immediately recognize the other types on his cellblock: the contorted face and broken gait of Chaser, strung out on psychotropics; the slumping, defeated Albert Brown as he shuffles outside his deserted cell; the drunken, screaming Hammerhead, guzzling hootch as he runs from the hacks. The situations described by Hassine are everyday occurrences in many prisons: the swag men brazenly hawking sandwiches to their customers; the gruesome tasks of the "meat wagon crews" loading victims of drug overdoses and violence onto their gurneys; "the inmate's dilemma" of whether a victim should fight a burglar caught ransacking one's cell.

Hassine overcomes part of the problem of external validity by giving the reader a panoramic view of modern prison life rather than a retrospective self-portrait. *Life Without Parole* captures the atmosphere of crushing boredom, endless routine, mindless amusement, and occasional gripping fear that almost every inmate experiences every moment in every American prison.

Deprivation or Importation?

Correctional researchers have long recognized that a distinctive inmate subculture—with separate norms, values, attitudes, beliefs, and language—flourishes in prison (see Carroll [1974] 1988, 1977; Clemmer 1940; Goffman 1961; Irwin [1970] 1987; Irwin and Cressey 1962; Jacobs 1977; Sykes 1958). Strong evidence of this prisoner subculture is found in Chapter 1 ("How I Became a Convict"), especially when Hassine notes how jailhouse slang unifies inmates into "one big clan," and in Chapter 4 ("The Underground Economy"), where he comments on the "Inmate Code of Conduct" in Graterford.

There is a heated debate among scholars about the origins of this subculture. Those supporting the "deprivation model" argue that the "pains of imprisonment"—including the losses of liberty, material goods and services, heterosexual relationships, autonomy, and personal security—contribute to the formation of a peculiar inmate society with well-defined prisoner roles (see Clemmer 1940; Goffman 1961; in particular Sykes 1958). Hassine recalls that he received his first misconduct charge in Graterford because he missed "one of life's simplest pleasures: a fresh cooked burger." He purchased ten pounds of frozen ground beef from a swag man, a convict who specializes in providing goods and services to prisoners who desire the material comforts of the outside world. Deprivation theorists argue that complex inmate societies, of which swag men are only a small part, have an "indigenous origin" (Sykes 1958): the hardships of confinement lead to the development of a criminogenic subculture found only within prisons.

Proponents of the "importation model" counter that the inmate subculture is not a response to the isolation and deprivations of imprisonment, but instead is brought into the prison from the streets (see Carroll [1974] 1988, 1977; Jacobs 1977; in particular Irwin [1970] 1987; Irwin and Cressey 1962). The importation model views pre-prison experiences as the most important factors shaping the development of prison subcultures. For example, Irwin and Cressey (1962) argue that prison subcultures and prisoner roles for the most part are not adjustments to the deprivations of confinement; rather they are composites of various criminal and conventional street identities that are imported into the prison. As one example, Hassine is a square john to the other convicts because of the law-abiding, middle-class values and conventional identity he carried with him from the outside world.

The consensus among most correctional scholars is that the importation model is the superior explanation for the inmate subcultures found in modern American prisons (Wright 1994). In the 1960s and early 1970s, correctional reforms and federal court decisions eased some of the pains of imprisonment, making it easier for prisoners to retain their street identities and lifestyles (Carroll [1974] 1988, 1977; Jacobs 1977). Among the correctional reforms, Carroll and Jacobs note that the liberalization of visitation, telephone, and mail privileges, and the permission to wear street clothes and hairstyles, to decorate their cells, and to bring television sets and radios into prisons enabled inmates to maintain close contact with the outside world and to preserve their pre-prison, street personalities. United States Supreme Court decisions extended the freedom of religion to prisoners (in *Cooper v. Pate*, 1964), virtually abolished the censoring of inmate mail by prison officials (in *Procunier v. Martinez*, 1974), and extended limited constitutional protections to inmates (in *Wolff v. McDonnell*, 1974), further reducing the isolation of prisoners from society.

Although Hassine describes the deprivations of imprisonment—including the losses of heterosexual love, possessions, privacy, peace and quiet, and personal security—*Life Without Parole* offers far stronger support for the importation model. Hassine observes that in the early 1980s the "ghetto evils of the decaying American inner city" were compressed into Graterford. He notes that almost overnight gang bangers, drug addicts and dealers, the homeless, the mentally ill, and juvenile offenders poured into the penitentiary, disrupting prison life and routines. The violent, addictive, acquisitive, disorganized lifestyles of the new inmates especially offended the Old Heads, who longed for the good old days when the "*outside world was kept outside.*"

Hassine's comments in Chapter 6 ("Race Relations in Prison") about prison gangs bolster the importation position. (For a sociological analysis of the effect of street gangs in Stateville Penitentiary, see Jacobs 1977.) He mentions that inmate organizations among both African Americans and whites are dominated by gangs that once roamed the streets. Philadelphia neighborhood gangs bearing specific street names—e.g., the 10th Street Gang—govern interactions among African Americans at Graterford; outlaw motorcycle gangs from rural Pennsylvania organize white prisoners. Prison gangs import their roles, organizational structures, and leadership styles directly from the streets. In many American prisons today, inmates must turn to gangs for drugs and other contraband or for simple protection (see Fong, Vogel, and Buentello 1992).

Correctional practitioners and researchers now recognize that the imposing prison walls that surround institutions like Graterford are surprisingly permeable. While prison walls, fences, and towers still prevent the inside world from getting outside, they can no longer prevent the outside world—with its diverse attractions, diversions, and problems—from getting inside.

The Penal Harm Movement

Although correctional reforms and court decisions dramatically lessened the deprivations experienced by prisoners in the 1960s and early 1970s, the pains of imprisonment have since worsened. Some scholars claim that conservative politicians are spearheading a "penal harm movement" in America today, with the intention of increasing the misery associated with punishment (Clear 1994; Cullen 1995; Simon 1993; Tonry 1995). While Cullen reminds us that corrections has always been a "mean-spirited enterprise," he contends that the recent popularity of "three-strikes-and-you're-out" laws (that mandate life sentences for third-felony convictions) and the reappearance of chain gangs in Alabama are "symbolic" indicators of the rise of penal harm. More substantively, Clear (1994, p. 50) documents that since 1972 "every state altered its penal policy in the direction of greater punitive severity" through such measures as the restriction or abolition of parole release and/or the implementation of mandatory sentencing laws.

Because the penal harm movement specifically targets predatory street crime and the crack cocaine epidemic, massive numbers of minority-group, drug-addicted, urban-underclass offenders have entered Graterford and other American prisons during the last decade. (For academic accounts of these developments, see Clear 1994; Simon 1993; Tonry 1995.) For prison administrators, this means coping with overcrowding while also stretching institutional programs and services beyond their limits to meet the extensive needs of a diseased, drug-addicted, and illiterate inmate population. Prison officials often must meet these new demands under the pressure of budget freezes imposed by state legislatures.

Life Without Parole superbly details the practical effect of the penal harm movement on the lives of inmates (see in particular Chapter 3, "Prison Violence"). By the mid-1980s, prison officials apparently lost control of Graterford to rival inmate gangs; cellblocks were filled with drugs, violence, and corruption. While assigned to the meat wagon crew, Hassine served as a medic on the frontline of penal harm. Although he argues (in Chapter 4, "The Underground Economy") that the confrontation between Double D and Rocky replaced disorganized, "tribal" gang violence with a united "Kingdom of Inmates," recent events (see Appendix B, "A State Tries to Rein in a Prison Awash in Drugs") suggest that this period of relative tranquility in Graterford was shortlived.

Through its impact on prison overcrowding (see Clear 1994), the penal harm movement has increased the deprivation suffered by virtually every inmate in America. In Chapter 13 ("Prison Overcrowding"), Hassine offers a personal account of the suffering he has experienced from double-celling. Some prisons are now triple- and even quadruple-celling inmates or requiring prisoners to sleep barracks-style in warehouses, gymnasiums, or auditoriums. One shudders when imagining the problems that inmates confront under these circumstances.

In an attempt some years ago to articulate a "new ideology" for punishment, the eminent correctional scholar John Irwin sensibly argued:

> Those convicted of serious crimes must be punished and imprisoned—knowing that imprisonment itself is very punitive, we need not punish above and beyond imprisonment. This means that we need not and must not degrade, provoke, nor excessively deprive the human beings we have placed in prison. (1980, p. 248)

By promoting prison overcrowding and its related evils, the penal harm movement has clearly extended degradation, provocation, and deprivation well beyond the act of imprisonment to the daily *conditions* of confinement.

The Penology of Desperation

Criminal justice theorists and philosophers of punishment endlessly debate the appropriate rationales for criminal justice processing. For example, in a famous conceptualization of criminal procedure, Packer (1968) distinguishes between the crime control and the due process models. The crime control model emphasizes the efficiency of convictions, the presumption of guilt, and the validity of the coercive power of the state over the offender; due process emphasizes the reliability of convictions, the presumption of innocence, and the strict protection of individual rights through the limitation of state power. Philosophers of punishment argue *ad nau-seam* about the relative merits of retribution (matching the severity of punishments to the seriousness of crimes), rehabilitation (implementing treatment strategies and programs to reform individual offenders and to prevent future crimes), deterrence (using threatened or actual punishments to convince persons not to commit future crimes), and incapacitation (preventing crime in the larger society through the use of punishment to remove criminals from circulation in free society) as the rationales for correctional policies and programs.

Some recent commentators claim that these older models and rationales have little relevance to the current operations of prisons. Rutherford (1993) contends that a bureaucratic "expediency model"—that emphasizes smooth management and pragmatic efficiency through adopting a procedure-based, mechanistic, emotionally detached administrative style—guides correctional thinking today. Feeley and Simon (1992) refer to this administrative approach as the "new penology." These authors argue that the expediency model contained in the new penology is a practical response to the immediate pressures of overcrowding, violence, and disorganization in prisons.

Hassine's runaway train analogy (Chapter 17, "Conclusion") offers a far more disturbing image of current correctional operations. He believes that the problems in modern prisons have become so grave that prison administrators are simply "crisis-control managers" whose primary goal is to "avert a catastrophe" in a "renegade bureaucracy." Overcrowded cellblocks ruled by gangs and filled with drugs and violence mean that prisoners and staff alike are only concerned about "how they are going to survive this madness." The implication is that in the last few years, correctional policy has rapidly moved from some variation of crime control, due process, retribution, rehabilitation, deterrence, and incapacitation, through expediency, to mere survival.

Sadly, I believe that Hassine's observations are correct. It appears that many prisons in the United States are in such a condition of turmoil that many correctional officials are now more concerned about serving their tours of duty with their minds and bodies intact than seriously considering any abstract models or rationales of punishment. Because new disasters and outrages occur almost every day, prison officials must constantly improvise and adjust their actions to suit each new crisis. There is no game plan, no blueprint, and certainly no hope in all of this. After all, expediency is still a model, but survival is only an instinct.

The penal harm movement embraced by the public and politicians in the outside world has led to a "penology of desperation" on the inside. It is of urgent importance that Americans reconsider the policies that have increased the harms inflicted on prisoners, if not for captives like Victor Hassine, then at least for their captors.

References

Abbott, Jack Henry. 1982. *In the Belly of the Beast: Letters from Prison*. New York: Vintage.

Babbie, Earl. 1992. *The Practice of Social Research*. 6th ed. Belmont, CA: Wadsworth.

Brownmiller, Susan. 1975. *Against Our Will: Men, Women, and Rape*.

Carroll, Leo. (1974) 1988. *Hacks, Blacks, and Cons: Race Relations in a Maximum Security Prison*. Prospect Heights, IL: Waveland.

———. 1977. "Race and Three Forms of Prisoner Power: Confrontation, Censoriousness, and the Corruption of Authority." Pp. 40-53 in *Contemporary Corrections: Social Control and Conflict*, edited by C. Ronald Huff. Beverly Hills, CA: Sage.

Clear, Todd R. 1994. *Harm in American Penology: Offenders, Victims, and Their Communities*. Albany, NY: State University of New York Press.

Clemmer, Donald. 1940. *The Prison Community*. New York: Holt, Rinehart and Winston.

Cullen, Francis T. 1995. "Assessing the Penal Harm Movement." *Journal of Research in Crime and Delinquency* 32: 338-58.

Denzin, Norman K. 1989. *The Research Act*. 3rd ed. Englewood Cliffs, NJ: Prentice-Hall.

Feeley, Malcolm M. and Jonathan Simon. 1992. "The New Penology: Notes on the Emerging Strategy of Corrections and Its Implications." *Criminology* 30: 449-74.

Fong, Robert S., Ronald E. Vogel, and Salvador Buentello. 1992. "Prison Gang Dynamics: A Look Inside the Texas Department of Corrections." Pp. 57-77 in *Corrections: Dilemmas and Directions,* edited by Peter J. Benekos and Alida V. Merlo. Cincinnati: Anderson.

Genet, Jean. (1949) 1964. *The Thief's Journal.* New York: Grove.

Goffman, Erving. 1961. *Asylums: Essays on the Social Situation of Mental Patients and Other Inmates.* Garden City, NY: Anchor.

Ianni, Francis A. J. 1972. *A Family Business: Kinship and Social Control in Organized Crime.* New York: Russell Sage Foundation.

Irwin, John. (1970) 1987. *The Felon.* Berkeley: University of California Press.

———. 1980. *Prisons in Turmoil.* Boston: Little, Brown.

Irwin, John and Donald R. Cressey. 1962. "Thieves, Convicts, and the Inmate Culture." *Social Problems* 10: 142-55.

Jackson, George. 1970. *Soledad Brother.* New York: Bantam.

Jacobs, James B. 1977. *Stateville: The Penitentiary in Mass Society.* Chicago: University of Chicago Press.

Packer, Herbert L. 1968. *The Limits of the Criminal Sanction.* Stanford, CA: Stanford University Press.

Rutherford, Andrew. 1993. *Criminal Justice and the Pursuit of Decency.* Oxford, England: Oxford University Press.

Shaw, Clifford R. 1930. *The Jack-Roller: A Delinquent Boy's Own Story.* Chicago: University of Chicago Press.

Simon, Jonathan. 1993. *Poor Discipline: Parole and the Social Control of the Underclass, 1890-1990.* Chicago: University of Chicago Press.

Solzhenitsyn, Aleksandr I. 1974. *The Gulag Archipelago.* New York: Harper and Row.

———. 1975. *The Gulag Archipelago, Two.* New York: Harper and Row.

———. 1976. *The Gulag Archipelago, Three.* New York: Harper and Row.

Sutherland, Edwin H. 1937. *The Professional Thief.* Chicago: University of Chicago Press.

Sykes, Gresham M. 1958. *The Society of Captives: A Study of a Maximum Security Prison.* Princeton, NJ: Princeton University Press.

Tonry, Michael. 1995. *Malign Neglect: Race, Crime, and Punishment in America.* New York: Oxford University Press.

Whyte, William Foote. 1943. *Streetcorner Society*. Chicago: University of Chicago Press.

Wright, Richard A. 1994. *In Defense of Prisons*. Westport, CT: Greenwood.

Cases

Cooper v. Pate 378 U.S. 546 (1964).

Procunier v. Martinez 416 U.S. 396 (1974).

Wolf v. McDonnell 418 U.S. 539 (1974).

APPENDICES

Mr. Smith Goes to Harrisburg

I n April of 1989, I was transferred to the State Correctional Institution at Camp Hill, where I served six months of my life sentence. Camp Hill was the "jewel" in Pennsylvania's correctional crown, and it housed some 3000 inmates. It was a fenced institution next to the main offices of the Pennsylvania Department of Corrections outside the state capital of Harrisburg.

At that time, Richard C. Smith was Camp Hill's Deputy Superintendent of Operations, the youngest official in Pennsylvania history to be appointed to this position. He had worked his way up through the ranks, starting as a correctional officer at Pittsburgh in 1977. His meteoric rise seemed to guarantee that he would become a commissioner in the not too distant future.

However, 1989 proved to be a particularly disastrous year for Mr. Smith and the Department of Corrections. On October 25th, Camp Hill suffered the longest and most costly riot in Pennsylvania history. For four days, hundreds of angry, desperate inmates commandeered and controlled the entire facility. Many inmates and guards were savagely beaten and raped. The prison was almost completely destroyed before the Pennsylvania State Police managed to regain control.

Shortly after the riot, Mr. Smith was fired and his promising career came to an abrupt end. On February 21, 1990, the Pennsylvania Senate Judiciary Committee conducted a public hearing to investigate "recent incidents at Pennsylvania State Correctional

Institutions." Mr. Smith was asked to give sworn testimony at the hearing, which was conducted in Harrisburg, Pennsylvania.

The following are excerpts from the 162-page official transcript of Mr. Smith's testimony, in which he gave an insider's view of what happened just before the Camp Hill riot. For years I was of the opinion that nobody in the Department of Corrections would ever acknowledge the problems in the state's prison system. That is, until Mr. Smith came to Harrisburg. In his testimony he graphically outlined incident after incident of corruption, violence, drug dealing, and incompetence. This disturbing account will give outsiders a clearer sense of the grim realities of prison life.

The following is drawn from sworn testimony before an official committee of the state legislature by a high-ranking prison administrator. When it comes to prison conditions, Richard C. Smith knows what he's talking about.

EXCERPTS OF THE TRANSCRIPT OF PROCEEDINGS
BEFORE: SENATOR J. GREENLEAF, CHAIRMAN
               SENATOR JOHN D. HOPPER
               SENATOR JOHN J. SHUMAKER
DATE: FEBRUARY 21, 1990, 9:30 A.M.
PLACE: CAPITOL BUILDING
               HARRISBURG, PENNSYLVANIA

Editor's Note: Because Mr. Smith gave verbal testimony, these excerpts may be confusing to read. Editorial changes have been made to clarify his apparent meaning, and these are indicated by parentheses and italics. The names in the transcript are a matter of public record, but all names except for Mr. Smith's have been deleted.

Mr. Smith refers to various ranks in the prison organization without explaining them. The "commissioner" is in charge of the entire state prison system, while the "superintendent" (or "warden") is in charge of a single prison. "Deputy superintendents" have broad responsibilities within the entire institution and are referred to as "deputies." "Majors," "lieutenants," and "sergeants" are the ranks above "corrections officers" (or guards).

CHAIRMAN GREENLEAF: We will begin our Senate Judiciary Committee hearing on the Camp Hill riots. Our witness today will be Mr. Richard C. Smith.

Thank you for being here today, Mr. Smith, and I appreciate your time and attendance. Would you raise your right hand and be sworn?

RICHARD C. SMITH, being sworn, testified as follows. . . .

Editor's Note: To begin his testimony, Mr. Smith described his professional background and his rise through the ranks from Pittsburgh to Camp Hill in 1986. He discussed the explosion of Pennsylvania's prison population from 8,200 inmates in 1980 to over 20,000 in 1989 and the Department's monumental efforts to expand existing prisons and open new ones in order to house all the new inmates. Then he described the general chaos that ensued from this population explosion. At this point, we pick up his testimony.

. . . So I came to Camp Hill. While I was at Camp Hill, I thought I had seen it all at Pittsburgh. And what I am about to lay out to you in no way exemplifies or shows the type of staff at Camp Hill. But there were problems. The vast majority of people at Camp Hill are good, hard-working people. But I think you need to know what we were dealing with in Camp Hill. You want to know what happened, what caused it, where our focus was. You need to know some of these things.

. . . There was a corrections officer, October 29, 1986, had just got out of the hospital for open-heart surgery, just finally reported back to work. Another officer beats him up inside the institution, outside the control desk. He is terminated. July 15, 1987, another officer was caught smuggling contraband through the rear gate into the institution. Terminated.

Q: What kind of contraband?

A: Sneakers, tennis shoes, coffee, chewing gum, letters being smuggled in and out for the inmates, nuisance-type contraband. May 29, 1987, we set up a sting operation in cooperation with the Pennsylvania State Police, busted this officer at the Harrisburg bus station. Criminal attempt to deliver methamphetamine, a half a pound, payment of 500 dollars cash, and a half ounce of marijuana for personal use, in return for smuggling the half pound of methamphetamine into the State Correctional Institution at Camp Hill for an inmate.

October 6, 1987, an officer permitted one inmate in the RHU [*Restricted Housing Unit, or the Hole*] to beat another inmate for two solid hours. Obviously he [*the officer*] was inattentive or asleep. That inmate was later transferred to the State Correctional Institution at Dallas and a short time later committed suicide. Tragic.

Corrections tailoring tradesmen instructor, October 14, 1987. A captain at Camp Hill came in the institution late, I think it was 6:30 or 7:00 at night, runs into my office and says an inmate just ran in the captain's office and says that a staff member just raped him. Yes, it happened.

I had to go to Civil Service Commission when we finally defended the case, on the [*witness*] stand for seven hours to defend it. Where should the security office, the security lieutenant, and everybody at Camp Hill, where should their focus be? It should be on the 25, 26 hundred inmates. But these types of things happen day after day after day. And the frightening thing to me about Camp Hill, when you compare Camp Hill and Pittsburgh, is as a lieutenant you constantly get information in the institution.

At Pittsburgh, 5 percent maybe of what you heard when you investigated it was true. At Camp Hill, 99 percent of what you heard when you investigated it turned out to be true. Major A used to come into my office and say, "Listen to this now." And I knew as soon as he had that look on his face, it was like, God, we're into it again. What did someone do now? Female officer, December 23, 1987, union official at the institution, sent an inmate money and material goods on several occasions; gave an inmate personal photographs, phone number, address; witnessed a sexual incident while on duty in the visiting area at Camp Hill, failed to report it; wrote letters to an inmate while on duty on 14 occasions; reported off sick to go visit an inmate at Rockview; visited an inmate 13 times at another state correctional institution. Terminated. . . .

A dental assistant in Camp Hill, March 29, 1988, [*had a*] positive urine screen in the institution on duty for cocaine, arrest by York Police Department, possession with intent to deliver a half ounce of cocaine, late for work, found asleep in his car in the Camp Hill parking lot. This is what we were dealing with.

Union official, corrections carpenter trades instructor, August 22, 1988, permitted outside inmate detail to consume sausage patties at work. Sounds trivial. Those of you who have been around Camp Hill for a while know that the abattoir, the meat processing plant up across Lisburn Road, handles all the meat for the state prison system, permits the inmates to smuggle sausage patties and steaks into the institution through the main gate.

The same time this happens, this person was found to have a box of ammunition and alcoholic beverages in his van at the rear gate at Camp Hill.

I have to be honest with you. I dropped the ball there. We had the one escape since Superintendent D came in, we had the one escape, the guy was found running through Sheepford Crossing, and we were trying to deal with that. When this information came to me about [the official] having his car unlocked and ammunition on the seat, and alcohol and all that, it was just too much going on, and it was untimely. We didn't deal with it.

We had an officer, May 16, 1988, terminated, refused to participate in mandatory CPR [cardiopulmonary resuscitation] training, intentionally failed the CPR examination. Now you are sitting there as an administrator and you are saying, "Wait a minute, this is a people business." This is like, to us, this was like a policeman, but, "I'm not going to help anybody. I'm not going to do CPR on anybody." And [he should] realize, if you are a staff member and you are taught to do CPR, maybe another staff member will have a heart attack. That happens in prison just like it does in the Senate and the House and anywhere in the Capitol. It happens. This guy admitted, "I purposely failed the test." . . .

Food-service instructor, January 25, 1987—I realize I'm leaving a lot out, I'm hitting the ones that I think are serious cases. . . . I'm in the institution at 1:00 in the morning, checking on the officers on the night-turn shift: "How is it going, any problems?" They bring this guy in. They caught him breaking into the food-service manager's office. What is in there? He's bored so he broke in and was rifling through [the manager's] desk and his files, broke the window out. [This was a] staff member.

Activities department staff member—and listen to this one because you want to know why the riots occurred and what was going on at Camp Hill—activities department, September 22, 1989. We received allegations that this staff member was embezzling funds from the Jaycees [*the inmate chapter of the Junior Chamber of Commerce*] and the Lifers association in the institution. We turned it over to internal affairs in the Commissioner's office.

They dragged their feet on it, dragged their feet on it. We are trying to figure out what's going on. Finally the guy knows he's under investigation, he's dirty, he can't take the pressure any more, goes to Deputy C, and confesses. So we have to close the Lifers and the Jaycees. If you know anything about prisons, you know that the inmate organizations are very critical. You've got to watch them closely, make sure they go by their constitutions. Who is supposed to be monitoring the inmate organizations? Staff. [*But*] staff is dirty who's supposed to be watching them. . . .

Shortly after I'm assigned to Camp Hill, there is an officer. Staff comes in and tells me that an officer was fighting an inmate in the day room. Why? We find out because they bet over the Super Bowl. He lost to the inmate. He was supposed to pay him ten packs of cigarettes and only paid him eight, so he's fighting with the inmate in the day room. He gets a ten-day suspension. Again, are we popular for these moves? No. But it's my feeling that, if officers are dealing with inmates that way, somebody is going to get killed. . . .

Major A gets offended because I say to him repeatedly, "Major, is this a kiddy camp?" I'm not used to operating like this. At Western Penitentiary you can't deal with inmates like this. . . .

Another food-service instructor, vice president of the union. We find out [*he*] smeared peanut butter in a black inmate's hair, placed flour and jelly in two black inmates' hair in the culinary department, rubbed chopped onions in a black inmate's face, conducted a mock hanging off a steam pipe under the guise of the Ku Klux Klan, verbally abused the black inmates, calling them "nigger hop," "little nigger," et cetera.

You should not have to deal with this as an administrator. You should be focused on the inmates. What are the criminals doing? That's what the focus should be on, but it's not. . . .

Labor foreman in the maintenance department, October 31, 1986, purposely jams his brakes on his truck [*and*] flips an inmate out over the front cab of the truck onto the ground. One-day suspension. Should not have to deal with these kinds of things.

Food-service instructor, October 8, 1987, man engaged in and permitted a raw-egg fight—an egg fight, like *Animal House*—with his inmate detail in the culinary department at Camp Hill. Where should the focus be? It should be on the inmates. You shouldn't have to deal with this. Staff stealing from the commissary, it goes on and on and on and on.

An officer given a written reprimand June 27th, 1988, engaging in horseplay with an inmate—body punching and wrestling in J-Block. Who was the officer? This was the officer that was initially assaulted on Wednesday, October 25, 1989, at Camp Hill *[the day the riot started]*.

What did I tell you earlier? You can't deal with inmates like that. You can't horseplay with them, grab them, throw them down, wrestle with them. Somebody is going to get hurt. This is the same officer the first guy hit at Camp Hill *[riot]*.

Health-care administrator at Camp Hill. One of the issues on the riots at Camp Hill was the family day visits. The danger with the family day visits . . . *[was that]* visitors were permitted to come in with large picnic coolers of food. . . . *[There was no way]* staff could check that with the metal detector. The real incident that kicked this over the edge where we said we have got to change that policy, the hospital administrator authorized the family day visit inside the infirmary. Now, at least with the normal family day visits the food comes in, but the inmate is strip-searched by the officers before he actually goes back into the main prison compound.

In this incident the food was permitted in and went right inside the main compound. We searched the infirmary after that and found Pennsylvania lottery tickets, everything under the sun. We had to move on that policy. . . .

When I was on vacation I got a call from a captain that said an officer had just blown his brains out in the highway tower right behind the Department building. They blamed the administration for that. Why? Because the . . . local police department was patrolling the parking lot shortly after the daylight shift came on duty. The captain went out to check it out, asked the local policeman what the problem was. He said, "We're looking for a corrections officer who is accused of shoplifting on his way to work this morning." The captain had the officer relieved from the tower and asked him,

"What is going on? Are you having problems with the police? Are you under arrest?" I mean, we need to know these things.

I [*was challenged*] by a tradesman in the maintenance department who said that's none of our business. Yes, it is our business, you are in5- law enforcement. [*You*] are in the criminal justice community. Your life is an open book. It's not good enough just to be clean eight hours a day, [*then*] you can do whatever you want off duty. That's not what the citizens of the Commonwealth [*of Pennsylvania*] demand or what they deserve. That's what you signed up for. . . . If you don't like those kind of limitations being put on you, then you shouldn't work in corrections. . . .

Last on the staff-discipline issue, [*when I first*] came into Camp Hill . . . what is one of the first things that everybody runs and reports to me? All the money is stolen from the commissioned-officers' association. What is the first thing I say? "Well, where is it kept?" It's kept in the safe. "Who has the combination to the safe?" Only lieutenants and captains. The money is gone.

You shouldn't have to deal with this type of credibility of staff, especially management people, as an administrator. . . .

Q: Was that institution different than other institutions? Do the other institutions in the state have similar problems, other ones that you worked on?

A: I would say from my knowledge as Chief of Security, probably Graterford, and of course we didn't know Camp Hill until we got in there and started turning over the stones. But no, that is not typical of the other institutions, not to my knowledge.

Q: You think it might be typical of Graterford?

A: Absolutely, Senator. What I laid out for you gentlemen here today is mild compared to Graterford. . . .

Now we did have a lot of problems at Camp Hill with inmate discipline. . . . In September of 1989 before the riots, there were 327 misconducts filed by the officers. The total number of charges was 623. When they say charges, the officers have a laminated card that says, possession of contraband, refusing to obey an order, and charges like that. So on one misconduct there might have been four or five charges.

What was happening at Camp Hill was . . . there were 327 misconducts, 623 charges. Total number of guilty charges 438. Total number of not-guilty charges, 185.

We knew what was happening with the hearing examiner, in effect, was plea bargaining with the inmates. An inmate would come into a disciplinary hearing, the hearing examiner would say, "Well, I'll throw these three charges out if you plead guilty to refusing to obey an order." And, of course, the inmate knows he might get 30 days in the RHU if he agrees to that, versus 60 or 90.

But the point I wanted to make is that [it] simply was not under our control. We complained about that to the Department time after time after time, but he kept doing it. And he would be done at noon every day with all the misconduct hearings, but it's just not under our control. . . .

We implemented a new medical contract in June of 1989, but distribution of medications in Camp Hill rose from 75,000 doses of medication for inmates per month to 179,000 doses of medication per month by the end of September. . . . The nurses association, they want a change in the sick-line policy. Because, imagine the increase in work for the nurses when you go from issuing 75,000 doses a month to 179,000 doses a month. . . .

[A report] says that officers talked the inmates into signing up for sick lines en masse. That's not an inmate's statement, that's an officer's statement.

Interestingly enough, when I had the captain and lieutenant do that investigation, a number of the officers, who are named in this investigation as participating in that, are pumping the inmates up to subvert the two policies . . . it appears what [the officers] actually were doing was threatening me and telling me, "If you don't back off these policies, we're going to get people to sign up en masse and we'll make sure that you back off."

Do I think that they thought it would cause a riot? No. But again, it's a naive approach to corrections, and I think of that all as little pieces to the puzzle on why it crashed. . . .

Asbestos in the institution. I think it has to be addressed. In state government, I just saw on the news the other day, there was a DER [Department of Environmental Resources] building where they found friable asbestos. They immediately closed the building. I'm sure whoever [is in charge] is going to get outside contractors to come in and remove the asbestos. That conditions of confinement suit that was filed out of Western Penitentiary at Pittsburgh, part of that suit had to deal with asbestos.

At Camp Hill, and it's part of the reason and I'm sure you have asked everybody, you are going to ask me what I think should be done with the interior at Camp Hill. Camp Hill has a massive asbestos problem.

Just prior to the riots, again, what is the administration's thrust, what are we trying to deal with? We have sent, I think, eight staff members just prior to the riots at Camp Hill to a DPW *[Department of Public Welfare]* asbestos abatement and removal school. The *[prison]* population is going off the charts. Nobody is planning.

We try to do the planning for them. We are going to open the basements up in the 70-bed dorms. But what is the problem when we go down to open the basements up to 70 bed dorms? They are loaded with asbestos. So what do we have to do?

Now it's hurry up, it's a big crisis, to go into the basements . . . you can't use inmates for asbestos abatement, so what is the thrust in Camp Hill now? . . . Now not only are we going to open a 70-bed dorm, we have to take all the asbestos off. Now we've got to go in—it's a very complicated, cumbersome process. Borrow equipment from DPW, negative air machines, seal up the windows. We had to vent the negative air machines that we borrowed from DPW out through the B-Block basement window. We had to cut a window out. *[When we]* had the riot, that's how the B-Block basement got burned. Could we have done that another way? Probably. But when things are moving so fast and you are trying to deal with them, these things happen. You're trying to plan, you're trying to open dorms, you're trying to cut windows out, get the asbestos out. That's what is going on.

The day of the riots, October 25, 1989, what was I doing? I came in in the morning, had to pull all the acting safety officers together, pull all the files together on asbestos, because . . . now Camp Hill gets a conditions of confinement lawsuit.

. . . The Deputy Attorney General who is representing Camp Hill on the lawsuit is there to meet with us about this lawsuit, so we spend the entire day with him. In fact, when the incident first happened at the E gate, I was in B-Block showing him the friable asbestos in the plumbing chassis. These were all the things you have to deal with as an administrator and all the things that are going on. . . . The incident *[that started the riot]* happens at 3:00 in the afternoon at Camp Hill. . . .

The American Corrections Association recommends no new construction be over 500 beds and that doesn't mean like we have done in Pennsylvania, 500 beds times two, because everybody knows . . . once it's built, we are going to double-cell it. That means 500 beds. That is a manageable correctional institution. Staff knows the staff, staff gets to know the inmates. It is manageable. You start getting above a thousand and it's like a raging bull, and it is just raging and raging and raging out of control. You try as hard as you can, but you can't stay on top of it.

I guess when that happens you have to start making compromises. This staff has to . . . start making compromises, their security and their procedures, in order to just keep a relationship with them; in effect, stop them from taking over the institution. I suppose they would almost have to try to be buddies with them or something in order to stop them, [but] you don't have the manpower to use force to overtake them.

You never have a situation where . . . you have sufficient manpower at any time of the day where, if they want to take over, they are going to take it. That is a reality of corrections.

And I think that is also one of the problems that has happened at Camp Hill. And I know, if you had asked me six months ago if we would ever have 500 inmates in a rage like we did at Camp Hill, I would have probably said no way, because my experience up until the riots at Camp Hill have been, even when you had an incident at Pittsburgh or something, you would see 200 inmates. But when all the smoke cleared and you identified people, you find out it was these five or ten [perpetrators] and the other guys were just there milling around out of peer pressure.

Pennsylvania has never had a situation where it was 500 guys on a rampage. And . . . I think that affected the staff severely at Camp Hill, not just Camp Hill, but statewide, because we don't forget help is coming in every day to Camp Hill from all the other institutions. So they all know what happened, and that security blanket has been removed, although you always had it in the back of your mind as a corrections person that it could happen. It never happened, but now it happened. People went right through walls, people burnt half the jail down. That security blanket has been removed, and it's frightening. . . .

Appendix B

Editor's Note

During the editing of this book the State Correctional Institute at Graterford experienced a system-wide breakdown, a derailment. Hundreds of corrections officers and specialists who had never before been inside Graterford were brought in to help fix the problem. What these outsiders discovered when they explored Graterford for the first time was the "Kingdom of Inmates" which Victor Hassine has described in this book—and which they subsequently reported on in The New York Times article below.

A State Tries to Rein in a Prison Awash in Drugs

Reprinted from *The New York Times*, October 30, 1995
Matthew Purdy

GRATERFORD, Pa., October 26—In February, the Pennsylvania authorities paroled Robert Simon, despite his being a convicted killer and known prison drug user who had killed another inmate in self-defense.

Three months later, back on the street, Mr. Simon was accused of another killing, this time the shooting of a New Jersey police officer who had stopped him and a fellow motorcycle gang member in Gloucester County for a traffic violation.

When the authorities in Pennsylvania began looking into why Mr. Simon was set free, the trail led back to the state prison here, where officials say the case is another sign of the widespread drug trade, mismanagement, and possible corruption at the crowded maximum-security prison outside of Philadelphia.

In the view of state corrections officials, it was as if the prison had fallen into enemy hands. Last Monday, 650 state troopers and corrections officers from other prisons were deployed in a nighttime surprise assault on Graterford. During the next 72 hours, they searched all

3,500* inmates, the prison's staff, and its 1,700-acre grounds, looking for drugs and weapons. As a result, nine ranking officers at the prison retired or were transferred, and 21 inmates suspected of drug trafficking were moved to other prisons.

The shakedown, in which about 200 homemade weapons and more than 60 caches of drugs were seized, was unusual in scope. But the extreme action was an indication of the frustration many corrections officials and politicians feel at the constant battle to keep drugs out of prisons, especially as tougher laws are sending drug-addicted criminals away for longer sentences.

The question that prompted the raid—"Who runs the prison?" in the words of Martin F. Horn, Pennsylvania's Corrections Commissioner—is a common one for prison administrators. Corrections officials across the country say controlling prisons is becoming more difficult because of increasing inmate populations, harder-core prisoners, and tighter budgets. Earlier this month, inmates were ordered confined to their cells at federal prisons after uprisings at five sites.

The drug economy in prisons not only threatens peace among inmates but also dangles temptation before guards. In the last year at the federal prison in Atlanta, for example, several employees have been arrested on drug charges and there has been a spate of violence, including the first killing of a corrections officer at the prison since 1987.

(On Friday, federal prosecutors announced the indictments of four corrections officers, four inmates, and two others on charges of trying to smuggle marijuana, cocaine, and heroin into the Atlanta prison.)

"In large systems, it's almost a truism that you're going to have some drug trafficking," said a former Texas prison official and a consultant on prison conditions, Steve Martin. "But when it seeps into your security staff you have serious problems."

Governor Tom Ridge of Pennsylvania, who approved the search of Graterford, said, "The first thing we need to do is control the prisons, and we weren't in control of that one."

Officials said that in Mr. Simon's case a complete record of his prison misdeeds was not in his file when the parole decision was made. Inmates told a recent State Senate hearing that it was common practice among prisoners at Graterford to avoid punishment for infractions and to cover up evidence of drug use by paying officers to alter records.

At the hearing, an inmate who was a clerk at Graterford from 1992 to this January, Jonathan Brown, told the State Senate Judiciary Committee about officers' selling furloughs and other privileges, and about drug trafficking among officers. He said Mr. Simon paid officers to cover up his disciplinary infractions, though the allegations have not been proved and are under investigation.

"The fact that he was allegedly selling and using dope was not in his file," said the committee chairman, Senator Stewart J. Greenleaf.

Mr. Simon's case was just more evidence of trouble at Graterford, one of the largest state prisons in the country. Since 1989, 13 staff members have been arrested on charges of trying to smuggle drugs, 11 inmates have died of drug overdoses, and about 20 percent of the urine tests done on prisoners each month show signs of drug use.

In March, three inmates were found in a cell, all with hypodermic needles and all unconscious from drug overdoses, Mr. Horn said. They recovered, and one took another non-fatal overdose the next night.

Calling the drug trade in prison "enormously frustrating," Mr. Horn said it "gives the lie to everything we're trying to do in terms of rehabilitation."

The search had been planned since April by Mr. Horn and his staff without the knowledge of Graterford officials. In the raid, officers with drug-sniffing dogs removed inmates from their cells one at a time, searching the cells, strip-searching the inmates, and then moving to the next cell.

Officials say they might have found more drugs, but many inmates flushed them down toilets after hearing about the search.

"I suspect all of the bass and trout in the streams connected to that sewage system are jumping far out of the water," Mr. Ridge said.

Mr. Horn was realistic about the search's effect. "The minute we walk away from here, the inmates are going to start trying to figure out how to get drugs," he said.

Although few deny that Graterford has a drug problem, some prisoner advocates say the search, with all of its drama, had political motivations. The Simon case, which led to an overhaul of the state parole board, came less than a year after the release of a Pennsylvania inmate, Reginald McFadden, who went on to kill and rape on Long Island and in Rockland County, New York.

In last year's election, Mr. Ridge criticized his opponent, Lieutenant Governor Mark S. Single, for voting in favor of the McFadden parole as a member of the parole board.

Drug use at Graterford is both long-running and well-known.

"There was a period of time at Graterford that I smoked a joint when I woke up, at lunch, at dinner, and when I went to bed," said Kenneth Tervalon, 49, who was released in 1993 and says he has stopped using drugs.

Although just 10 percent of Pennsylvania's state prisoners are at Graterford, the prison accounts for 25 percent of inmate attacks on staff members and a third of inmate drug infractions, said Mr. Horn, who headed the parole system in New York State before becoming Commissioner in March.

Donald T. Vaughn, the superintendent at Graterford, said the drug problem was caused largely by its proximity to Philadelphia, which is 30 miles to the southeast. The drug market behind Graterford's 30-foot wall mirrors the city's.

Mr. Vaughn acknowledges that his staff might not have provided the "intense supervision" required for the prison. He said he had asked the corrections department for help in the past but had not yet received it.

Mr. Horn said he would leave Mr. Vaughn in charge.

With 85 percent of the inmates from Philadelphia or neighboring counties, there are frequent crowds in the visiting room, a key entry point of drugs in most prisons. Drugs packed in small balloons are passed mouth-to-mouth when inmates kiss female visitors, and inmates swallow them and pass them later. Although visitors are searched before coming in, they have been known to hide drugs in babies' diapers or in their own body cavities.

Inmates and others say Graterford has a more casual atmosphere than other prisons, which may contribute to the drug problem.

Prisoners are allowed to walk down the halls freely, not in straight lines under close supervision as is required in other prisons. And the number of volunteer workers—almost 400—gives inmates many chances to make contact with people from the outside.

"If you don't want to go to work, you just go out to the yard," said Steven Blackburn, an inmate for 12 years there until 1991. "Compared to a lot of other institutions around the state, Graterford is still considered loose."

Whatever that buys in inmate peace, it has its downside. On Au-gust 4, an inmate serving a life sentence for murder hid on a bread truck leaving the prison. He was recaptured 18 days later, but his escape was made possible because no one reported that he failed to show up for his job that day or that he was in the delivery area without authorization, Mr. Horn said.

Some inmates have been allowed to acquire enormous power. . . . A gang leader in Philadelphia has led Graterford's Muslim movement, officials said, controlling part of the prison's drug trade.

A prison guard, Lieutenant Cynthia Link, said that when the lights in the prison's mosque suddenly went out one night two years ago, the 100 inmates ignored her order to leave. Finally, one of them said, "Ms. Link, these people aren't going to move until [the gang leader] tells them to."

"I said, 'Well, go get [him], tell him I need him,'" Lieutenant Link recounted. He came, told the prisoners to leave, and they did. . . .

Editor's Note: As of this book's publication, the actual number of inmates at Graterford is over 4,000. At the time of this article, a portion of the prison had been shut down for repairs and emptied of inmates, which considerably reduced this figure.
